PLACES OF HEALTH AND AMUSEMENT

Liverpool's historic parks and gardens

Published by English Heritage, Kemble Drive, Swindon SN2 2GZ
www.english-heritage.org.uk
English Heritage is the Government's statutory adviser on all aspects of the historic environment.

Printing 10 9 8 7 6 5 4 3 2 1

Images (except as otherwise shown) © English Heritage, © English Heritage. NMR or
© Crown copyright. NMR.

First published 2008

ISBN 978 1 873592 91 5

Product code 51333

The Liverpool Culture Company has made a financial contribution towards the publication of this book.

British Library Cataloguing in Publication Data
A CIP catalogue record for this book is available from the British Library.

The National Monuments Record is the public archive of English Heritage. For more information,
contact NMR Enquiry and Research Services, National Monuments Record Centre, Kemble Drive,
Swindon SN2 2GZ; telephone (01793) 414600.

Photographs by James O Davies.
Graphics by Allan T Adams.
Brought to publication by Rachel Howard and René Rodgers, Publishing, English Heritage.
Edited by Sara Peacock.
Page layout by George Hammond.
Printed in the UK by Cambridge Printing.

Front cover
*Decorative ironwork gates,
Calderstones Park. These gates
originally stood at Bidston
Court, Birkenhead. They were
presented to the city of Liverpool
by Sir John Tilney in 1974.
[DP026154]*

Inside front cover
*Dramatic autumn colours in
Sefton Park. [DP030929]*

PLACES OF HEALTH AND AMUSEMENT

Liverpool's historic parks and gardens

Katy Layton-Jones and Robert Lee

The City of Liverpool

UNIVERSITY OF
LIVERPOOL

Liverpool
EUROPEAN
CAPITAL OF CULTURE

ENGLISH HERITAGE

Contents

Frontispiece
A tapestry of colour in the Japanese Garden, Calderstones Park.
[DP031270]

Acknowledgements

We would like to extend our grateful thanks to the following people who were instrumental in the publication of this book: Joseph Sharples made available his extensive knowledge of Liverpool; Dr Hazel Conway read and commented on the draft text; Adrian Allan and Tinho da Cruz of the University of Liverpool, Roger Hull and staff of the Liverpool Record Office, and staff of the Sydney Jones Library, University of Liverpool, kindly provided research materials; Allan T Adams (graphic illustrations) and James O Davies (photographs), both of English Heritage, provided new illustrations; and Colum Giles and Jenifer White (English Heritage), David Massey (University of Liverpool), Paul Scragg and Nigel Sharp (Liverpool City Council), and John Stonard (CABE Space) gave advice throughout the research project which produced the results on which this book is based.

Ironwork gates, Calderstones Park.
[DP031259]

Foreword

History has a way of repeating itself, and this is nowhere better illustrated than in attitudes to the provision of a healthy environment in our towns and cities. The need for public parks first became a matter of urgent policy in the 19th century, and the response was spectacular, especially so in Liverpool, one of the country's fastest growing cities but also one with extraordinary environmental problems. This book tells the story of how the city provided an impressive array of parks to meet contemporary needs. Economic decline and population loss in the latter half of the 20th century, however, led to neglect of the parks estate, and society lost sight of the arguments which had been used to justify its creation. The consequences of this collective amnesia have become increasingly evident, and there is now a new awareness, on the part of policy makers and the public, that good parks make good cities, just as the founders had set out a century and more ago.

Extremely difficult decisions are required to conserve and maintain public parks in highly competitive financial circumstances, but the strategic importance of open spaces is now widely recognised once again. The development by Liverpool City Council of a long-term strategy for its parks provides a framework for the management of its estate, and the City Council will be supported in its efforts by partner bodies such as English Heritage, CABE Space and the University of Liverpool, as well as by committed groups of Friends for whom access to clean and safe parks is a matter of everyday concern.

The years ahead will be challenging, but prospects are now better than they have been for many years. This book is offered as a way of increasing public awareness of the interest and importance of Liverpool's parks and the potential they have for enhancing people's lives and creating public enjoyment and well-being.

Lord Bruce-Lockhart, Chairman, English Heritage
Councillor Warren Bradley, Leader, Liverpool City Council
Professor Drummond Bone, Vice-Chancellor, University of Liverpool

CHAPTER 1

The origins of Liverpool's parks

The pleasant and salubrious situation of [Liverpool], the convenience of sea bathing, its amusements and the lively cheerful air which regularly pervades it, have of late years made it the resort also of Strangers of all descriptions, for the purposes of health and amusement.[1]

Liverpool's largest open space, the Mersey, has long guaranteed the city's international fame. Commerce, trade and heavy industry dominate the popular image of Liverpool and Merseyside as a whole. Yet the docks and warehouses that line the banks of the Mersey represent only one aspect of a vast and varied townscape. Beyond Liverpool's waterfront, across the city and throughout its suburbs, exists an extensive network of historic open spaces, parks, gardens, cemeteries and squares (Fig 1). Formal, naturalistic, dramatic or discreet – few British cities incorporate so extensive and varied a resource of public green spaces. Although these sites provide a welcome contrast to the hard-landscaping of the modern urban scene, they should not be considered as 'bubbles' within the city. They are, instead, an intrinsic part of the landscape and of the urban infrastructure. Liverpool's parks and open spaces have shaped and reflected the economic, social, political and cultural character of the city, their fortunes replicating closely those of Liverpool and its people. Over the past three centuries parks have improved the health of Liverpool's inhabitants and provided contact with nature and locations for collective recreation and amusement. Their history reflects the ebb and flow of international commerce, of population expansion in the 18th and 19th centuries and of economic decline in the 20th century. This relationship continues in the new millennium.

From their origins, urban parks and public gardens were designed as places for escape and recreation, but also as integral features of the townscape. Britain's provincial towns expanded during the 18th and 19th centuries as industry grew in scale and importance, attracting inward migration from the countryside. At first, the growing population was accommodated mainly within the old built-up areas of towns, leading in many cases to severe overcrowding. Outward growth soon followed and contact with the countryside was lost. As towns expanded it became

This view was taken from a balloon moored just south of Princes Park in 1859. It provides an unusually accurate view of Liverpool and Birkenhead in the mid-19th century. [Detail from J R Isaac, Liverpool in 1859. Formby Civic Society. Photograph courtesy of the University of Liverpool]

widely recognised nationally and locally that it was the poorest people who had the greatest need for access to open space and greenery, and that parks, pleasure gardens and recreation fields were to become important features of the new urban scene and valuable vantage points from which to appreciate it.

Liverpool shared fully in this urban flowering and for over 200 years it was one of the fastest growing towns in the country. Its population rose from about 6,000 in 1700 – the size of a small modern market town –

Figure 1 *Liverpool from the south: the built-up area is punctuated by the wide expanses of Sefton (centre foreground) and Princes Parks.* *[NMR 20440/020]*

to 78,000 in 1801 and, following boundary changes, to 518,000 in 1891. The immense social problems that attended such rapid growth became fully evident in the 19th century, and the creation of a network of parks was part of a far-sighted policy on the part of the Corporation of Liverpool to alleviate the worst social evils and to create a healthier city. The origins of this policy are, however, traceable in the 18th century.

Prospects and pleasure gardens

Liverpool in the 18th century was still a town on a human scale, easy to traverse and to appreciate as an entity. It was growing fast and it had its problems, many presaging those of the 19th century, but it was rightly regarded at the time as prosperous and, in part at least, handsomely built, with many new brick buildings in the London style. It supported a growing population dominated by wealthy mercantile families. Although primarily concerned with commerce, these families enjoyed the modern novelty of leisure time, and part of this time was spent socialising in the open air.

In towns like Liverpool before the late 18th century it was not difficult to find space for open-air amusement. For the whole population, rich and poor alike, the countryside, with its fields, commons and lanes, was immediately adjacent to the city (although not entirely open to all). Liverpool enjoyed enviable topography, for land rising from the Mersey offered extensive views over the town, the estuary and the far-off Welsh hills. Toxteth Park, in origin a royal hunting park on Liverpool's southern outskirts, provided an ideal vantage point from which to view the conurbation below. Whereas in estate parks, such as Calderstones and Croxteth, the views were rural and sought to provide a vision of ordered nature, the prospect over the town offered the excitement of a busy urban scene punctuated by new, grand public and commercial buildings, and busy shipping traffic on the river. The higher part of the Toxteth rise was used by many of Liverpool's inhabitants as an unofficial common and as a place for recreation and light industrial processing such as cloth tentering, which involved stretching lengths of cloth on tenter frames.

Many artists took advantage of its elevated position to gain a panoramic view of both the town and the river Mersey. As a result, this view of the town was reproduced in a number of paintings and prints of Liverpool (Fig 2).

The first deliberate provision of open space for recreation within Liverpool came in the early 18th century with the creation of Ranelagh Gardens, located on part of the site now occupied by the Adelphi Hotel, then on the fringe of the built-up area. Open between 1722 and the late 1790s, the gardens were modelled on the fashionable pleasure venue of the same name in Chelsea (Fig 3). In addition to a relatively conventional flower garden, Liverpool's Ranelagh incorporated a number of alcoves and arbours in which the wealthier personages of Liverpool and affluent visitors could congregate and socialise, while enjoying the polite pursuits of conversation, musical performances and, on occasional summer

Figure 2 *Throughout the 18th and 19th centuries, this view from Toxteth Park became one of the most widely recognised images of Liverpool. It was painted by numerous artists and an engraved version appeared in the* Illustrated London News *in October 1842. [Liverpool Record Office, Liverpool Libraries, G Pickering and J Sands, 1834,* Liverpool from Toxteth Park*]*

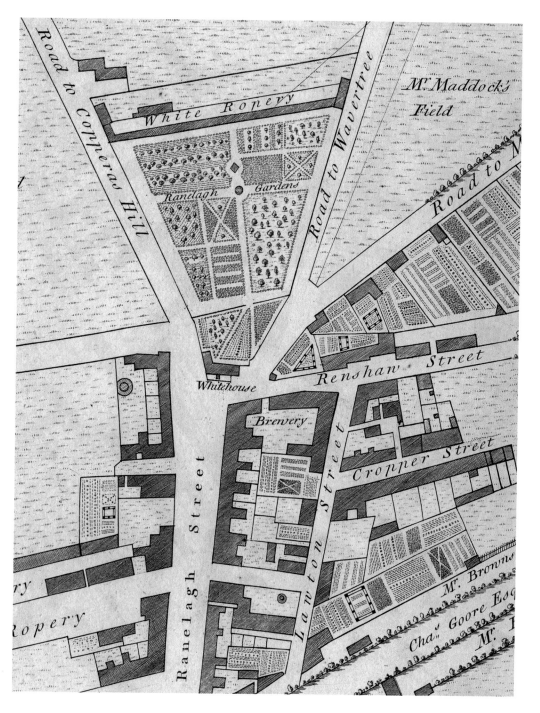

Figure 3 *A place for conversation and entertainment: Ranelagh Gardens, shown here on George Perry's map from 1769, were situated on the edge of the city. The modern Ranelagh Street takes its name from the gardens. [Liverpool Record Office, Liverpool Libraries, George Perry's Map of Liverpool, 1769]*

evenings, a fireworks display. Refreshments were served, making the gardens a place in which visitors could pass entire afternoons and evenings. They were open to the public for an admission charge, a measure which ensured a degree of social exclusivity. By visiting Liverpool's Ranelagh, the town's social elite emulated the habits and tastes of their metropolitan counterparts and, in so doing, presented themselves and their town as cultured, civilised and tasteful.

Behaviour in Ranelagh Gardens was heavily prescribed and the role of its patrons predominantly passive. The fishpond in the centre of the gardens was purely ornamental and the opportunities for physical exercise limited to the promenade or occasional dancing at special evening concerts. The scale and layout of the gardens reflected their function as a place of conversation and polite consumption. As the local antiquarian James Stonehouse described the site in 1852:

> The gardens were laid out very tastefully, with an abundance of flowers
> and shrubs … in the centre of the gardens there was a large fish-pond, in
> which there were great numbers of carp, tench and other fish. The
> gardens were a favourite resort of ladies in the afternoon, when the fish
> were fed by their fair visitors, much amusement being created by the
> struggles of the finny tribe to secure whatever was thrown to them.[2]

As well as Ranelagh Gardens, Liverpool offered a number of other walks where genteel society could take exercise and meet. Many were sited on the rising ground above the town to take advantage of the views over the river and of the good clear air which these locations enjoyed. Thomas Moss, writing in 1796, expressed the common view that

> The most healthful situations in the town are the higher parts, beginning
> near the top of Duke Street and continuing the northern direction
> towards Mount Pleasant and Everton. The higher parts of the west side
> of the town, bounded by Castle-Street, where they are not particularly
> crowded with inhabitants, from being purified by the frequent westerly
> winds from off the river, and the dry rocky foundation and sloping
> declivity, have always been healthful.[3]

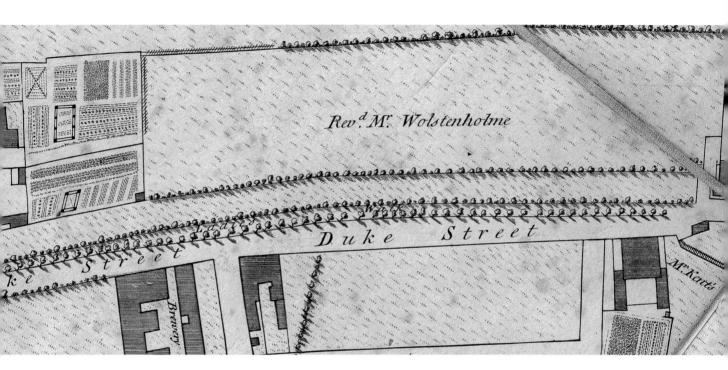

Figure 4 *One of Liverpool's earliest 'gardens' was Ladies Walk. A straight path through an avenue of trees, it ran adjacent to Duke Street and provided the opportunity to combine exercising with socialising. [Liverpool Record Office, Liverpool Libraries, George Perry's Map of Liverpool, 1769]*

Ladies Walk, adjacent to modern Duke Street, was situated in this 'healthful' area of the town (Fig 4). In 1797 Thomas Troughton, the chronicler of Liverpool, recollected it as 'a pretty walk … in which were four rows of trees, and from its elevated situation commanded the river, and all vessels passing to and from the town'.[4]

As the location of Ladies Walk illustrates, the area around the incline of Mount Pleasant was particularly popular for strolling and viewing the townscape and it was the site of the largest and most famous of Liverpool's early leisure grounds, St James' Walk, also known as St James' Mount and the Mount Gardens, (Fig 5). Begun in 1767 as a means of providing employment during a period of high bread prices, St James' Walk was free of admission charges and therefore represented a step forward in public space provision in Liverpool. As the author of *The Picture of Liverpool* explained in 1805, 'the whole belongs to, and is

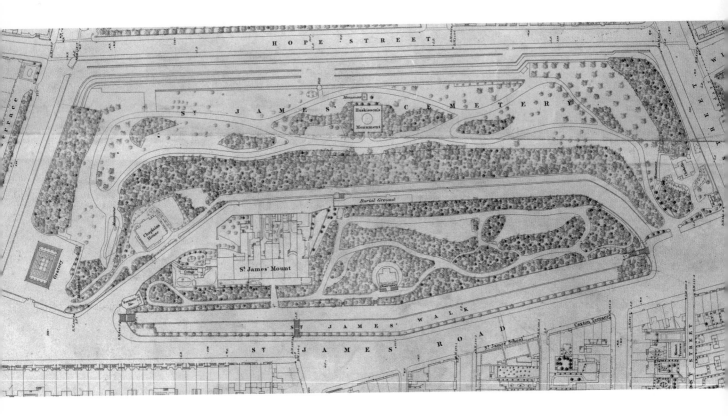

supported by, the Corporation, for public recreation: hence the public seem to consider it as their own, and respect it as such'.[5]

St James' Walk was situated on the edge of an old stone quarry. It was modestly landscaped, comprising a series of paths, shrubs, flowers and benches, and an observatory, situated on a small elevated mound. Although the gardens were replenished and maintained by the city for the benefit of the townspeople, its public status limited the Corporation's horticultural ambitions for the site. The initial layout was basic, orientated around paths rather than ornate structures, and later, in 1857, when it was decided that St James' Walk should be replanted, the Garden Committee accepted that 'plants for the Mount Gardens may be of an inferior kind to the Squares'.[6]

Figure 5 *St James' Walk was opened in 1769 and attracted visitors with its fine view of the town and river. [Liverpool Record Office, Liverpool Libraries, Ordnance Survey 5ft: 1 mile map, 1849]*

The location of St James' Walk provided the opportunity to view the vast majority of the town. Rather than denying the expanse of docks and the densely built warehouses, the park was advertised as a place from which to best take in the famous scene of Liverpool's mercantile character, and so to complement rather than conceal its commercial nature. The view was clearly valued by the Corporation and prompted one of the earliest attempts to actively preserve the character of the city's open spaces. As W Moss noted in his *Liverpool Guide* in 1796, 'as the Walk and the adjoining grounds belong to the Corporation, They have determined to prevent any buildings being erected in front, that may interrupt the prospect towards the river'.[7]

Unlike the common lands and churchyards that Liverpool's townsfolk had, for centuries, unofficially adopted for unregulated recreation, St James' Walk was designed specifically for public use. Its creation highlighted a new challenge for the Corporation: how to define and control behaviour in its public walks. Uses of public green space were progressively prescribed and unapproved uses curtailed. Commercial uses such as grazing livestock and market gardening were discouraged in these new 'leisure' facilities, while explicitly disruptive behaviour was increasingly prohibited. Activities deemed to be inappropriate, such as smoking, were banned and notice boards communicating the restrictions were installed at St James' Walk in the 1840s. At a similar time, the first staff dedicated purely to security were instated in St James' Walk on Sunday afternoons, and this provision was later upgraded to a police presence between 3pm and 9pm to 'prevent injury to the property'.[8] However, such regulations and special security measures did not isolate parks from the broader social, political and economic life of the city.

The Mount Gardens were clearly appreciated as a distinct urban feature and were acknowledged to be a general improvement to the city, enjoyed by both inhabitants and visitors alike. However, their linear form, limited extent and various regulations meant that they provided only a narrow range of opportunities for decorative landscaping and recreation. Moreover, the public status of the gardens made them less exclusive than might have been desired by the town's wealthier inhabitants.

Private space: garden squares

As Liverpool grew in wealth and size, those who could afford to escape
the dense and dirty city centre – principally the mercantile and
professional elite – relocated to the fringes of the town, some to the
heights of Mount Pleasant and Brownlow Hill, others to the southern
end of Duke Street and up the hill towards St James' Walk . This relatively
small area incorporated a large percentage of Liverpool's new urban
green spaces in the early decades of the 19th century, but unlike some
of the earlier walks and gardens many of these new spaces were reserved
for the exclusive use of the area's well-to-do inhabitants.

This mercantile exodus created Liverpool's great Georgian
townscape, where most of the houses were arranged in long terraces.
The largest of the terraced houses – for example, some in Rodney Street
– had small private back gardens screened by high brick walls. However,
the terrace layout in parallel streets was very restrictive, and a more
prestigious urban form – the garden square – offered far more potential
for the provision of open space. London, of course, was the model for
this type of development, while Edinburgh's New Town provided a more
recent exemplar. Garden squares were not common in Liverpool: Great
George Square, off Duke Street, was laid out by 1803, Abercromby
Square in 1815 (Fig 6), and Falkner Square as late as 1835, and their
rarity served to emphasise their prestige.

The concept of the garden square was simple: residents of the
houses around the square enjoyed exclusive or at least privileged access
to the central open area, with unauthorised entrance prevented both by
the railing in of the space and by the provision of keys to the residents
or fee payers. In 1843 the fee for non-residents to use the garden at
Abercromby Square was one guinea, rendering access to the gardens an
unaffordable luxury for the majority of Liverpool's labouring population.
Formally designed to incorporate paths, peripheral bedding and
occasionally larger structures such as summer houses, the garden
squares provided Liverpool's employer classes with their own private
parks. The gardens and houses were conceived as entire integrated
schemes, where the gardens could be viewed from the windows of the

Figure 6 *One of the new garden squares built in the
early 19th century, Abercromby Square was accessible
only to residents or annual subscribers. [DP031254]*

townhouses, providing an attractive aspect and the illusion of isolation from the encroaching town. As one guidebook described Great George Square in 1838, 'The houses, lofty and capacious, are the residences of some of the most respectable merchants. A spacious garden and shrubbery, surrounded by an iron railing, enlivens this square, and gives it a very pleasant appearance.'[9]

For those who could afford to inhabit the squares or pay the guinea fee, the gardens provided opportunities to exercise control over their immediate environment. Residents could request the introduction of new facilities or complain if they were dissatisfied with any aspect of the gardens' maintenance. Summer evening concerts, which had comprised much of the entertainment at Ranelagh Gardens a century before, were reintroduced by Liverpool's affluent society in the new private garden squares. In May 1839, the Corporation's Garden Committee, the body entrusted with the management of the squares and the Mount Gardens, received an application from a number of residents of Abercromby Square, 'respectfully requesting that the use of the Garden in the Square may be granted to Monsr de St Meurice of giving concerts a la Musard 2 evenings in each week during the months of June, July and August'.[10] Keyholders were also active in the more mundane issues of maintenance and security. When, in March 1843, it was found that 'many parties frequent the Gardens in the Squares without payment',[11] residents and subscribers were provided with lists of authorised users and requested to invigilate the park, reporting any trespassers to the authorities.

Interest in science: botanic gardens and zoological gardens

If for many people in the late 18th and early 19th centuries the principal use of gardens was as a place of entertainment and leisure, for others the primary interest was scientific. Great advances were being made in botanical studies, some the result of new discoveries in exotic parts of the world that were introduced to Britain via the port at Liverpool. Public interest in plants was widespread, reflecting a preoccupation with the

Enlightenment principle of understanding nature and applying its lessons for the improvement of society. For Liverpool, a town that aspired to rival London and other prominent towns as a place of culture, knowledge and taste, botanic gardens provided an opportunity to cultivate knowledge and learning as well as plants.

It was no coincidence that in 1802 Liverpool's first Botanic Garden was established on Myrtle Street on the fringe of the most prestigious residential area in the town as it expanded street by street up the hill. Laid out by the first curator, Mr John Shepherd, they were located within a triangular plot on a site known as 'Mosslake Fields', close to what was to become Abercromby Square. Having entered the grounds via a gatehouse on Garden Place (no longer in existence), visitors first encountered a garden dedicated to bog plants and a rockery, beyond which stood a large conservatory or 'hothouse' housing the most delicate tropical specimens (Fig 7). The largest portion of the gardens was given over to a large pond and extensive areas of herbaceous planting and grasses. The plants in this section were predominantly laid out in formal blocks, according to type, and so conducive to study: a kind of horticultural encyclopaedia.

Figure 7 *Extensive glasshouses were used to cultivate and protect the exotic specimens that constituted the main attraction of the original Botanic Garden on Myrtle Street. [From* Troughton, History of Liverpool *(1808), Liverpool Record Office, Liverpool Libraries Hq 942 721 TRO]*

However, serpentine paths were laid out along the periphery of the gardens to allow patrons to appreciate the aesthetic as well as scientific benefits of the project (Fig 8).

The Botanic Garden was promoted as a 'public institution' on a par with circulating libraries, philosophical societies and concert clubs. Like many similar institutions, the Botanic Garden was initially another 'subscriber democracy', funded by shareholders, who in addition to the share price of 12 guineas paid a 2-guinea subscription per annum. Membership extended only to subscribers' families and guests from outside Liverpool who could produce a letter of introduction. Consequently, the vast majority of the town's working population were excluded from entry.

A similar system of private subscription operated at Liverpool's Zoological Garden, where the prices in 1833 ranged from just over a shilling for a single annual ticket to three pounds and three shillings for a family of five (Fig 9). Entry for non-subscribers was a shilling a time, making the Zoological Garden more accessible than the Botanic Garden and garden squares, but nevertheless a socially exclusive place of resort. Little is known about the management of the Zoological Garden. Unlike the botanic collection, it was primarily a place of diversion and entertainment. Musical performances also attracted visitors, as 'Mr Stubbs Band' performed every Monday and Friday throughout the summer. Still, it was the animals, such as pelicans, bears, elephants and monkeys, that provided the main attractions, with the grounds being laid out with paths, shrubs and a lake so as to most effectively display the menagerie. As a guide to the gardens published in 1837 explains

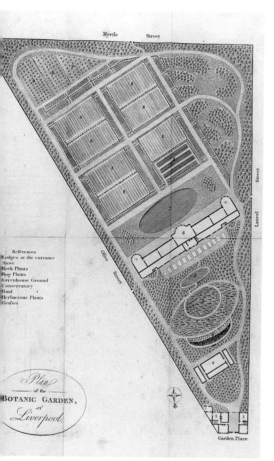

Figure 8 *As well as a living museum of horticultural specimens, the Myrtle Street Botanic Garden was a place for light exercise and recreation. The layout of the grounds, incorporating paths, ponds and flowerbeds, made it an attractive destination for tourists and locals alike. [From J Shepherd,* Catalogue of Plants in the Botanic Garden at Liverpool *(1808), Liverpool Record Office, Liverpool Libraries H580 74 SHE]*

> On leaving the Bear Pit, and turning to the left, it is a delightful promenade along the terrace walk, and by resting a moment at the arbour which terminates the walk, the visitors obtain a fine bird's-eye view of the whole grounds; after which, descending the path from the terrace to the lower grounds, and turning to the left, they arrive at the Pond and Rockery; in which are a pair of American Summer Ducks.[12]

Figure 9 *Liverpool's first zoological garden displayed animals and plants within a landscape embellished by water features and serpentine paths. [Liverpool Record Office, Liverpool Libraries, LIC 282]*

By the start of the Victorian era, Liverpool had achieved a great deal in the provision of private open space and of specialist, scientific gardens. However, the character of the town was changing rapidly, and in the new era the nature and extent of its open spaces were becoming glaringly inadequate. The periphery of Liverpool had crept steadily outwards, led by a demand among the city's wealthiest citizens for large residential properties away from the pollution and noise of the city centre. The garden squares around Mount Pleasant and Brownlow Hill were slowly abandoned by the wealthy. As Liverpool's green hinterland was developed, cultivated and privatised, public access to substantial green space was eroded, leaving the inhabitants of the most densely populated areas near the Mersey increasingly isolated from the environmental benefits of open space. The formerly 'healthful' atmosphere of the higher ground above the town was ever-more polluted, with the result that by the 1830s St James' Walk was under-used and the Botanic Garden suffered from the direct effects of smoke as well as the gradual migration of its members further afield to the clean air of the leafy suburbs. Something radical and new was required to replace what had been lost.

Figure 10 *Princes Park: Joseph Paxton's central feature for the park was an ornamental boating lake. Although the Swiss chalet-style boathouse has fallen victim to arson, the lake remains a popular resort for locals and anglers. [DP030898]*

Private parks and public access

The first major initiative in addressing the expanding city's needs may not, with the benefit of hindsight, appear to have been radical, but it was nevertheless of great significance as a step on the road towards the provision of accessible open spaces. Liverpool's experiment – Princes Park, laid out between 1842 and 1844 to the south of the expanding city – was to provide an example to towns and cities across the country (Fig 10). The scheme was a mix of residential development and semi-public gardens on a large scale. Although heralded by many as a great asset to the city, for the first 80 years of its existence Princes Park did not belong to the people of Liverpool. Instead, the park was the archetypal 19th-century marriage of public philanthropy and private commercial interest.

Named after the Prince of Wales, and originally designed to include several impressive townhouse terraces as well as individual villas, Princes Park represented the epitome of fashionable living and set a standard to which many of the city's new middle classes aspired (Fig 11). It was unprecedented in its scale and ambition, for its total extent of approximately 69 acres dwarfed all previous park and garden schemes in the growing town: Abercromby Square and its houses would fit comfortably within a small corner of the park. As with Ranelagh Gardens a century earlier, the designers of Princes Park looked to London for a model, in this case, John Nash's prestigious Regent's Park, laid out between 1811 and 1826. The mechanism for speculative development, with housing complemented by a specially designed landscape, was central to Regent's Park, where Nash's building scheme was set within grounds influenced by the principles of Humphry Repton, and later his son, George (Fig 12).

In 1842 the local industrialist and town councillor Richard Vaughan Yates approached the Corporation regarding a residential park scheme on the site, but it declined involvement in the project. Consequently, Vaughan Yates undertook to proceed with the development privately. Although his plan to establish a joint-stock company to fund the park was never fully realised, the site was purchased from Lord Sefton for just over £50,000. The costs of creating the park and maintaining it were borne by private shareholders, who sought a return on their investment through the sale and lease of private residences around the perimeter of its grounds. This funding structure enabled the construction of a number of grand features previously reserved for large estate parks, with the result that the development was made considerably more attractive to potential residents who entertained high social aspirations. In a similar fashion to the smaller-scale gardens of Falkner and Abercromby Squares, Princes Park provided an attractive vista from the surrounding properties and a section of the land was reserved for residents, replicating the locked-gate system of the garden-square developments.

For the design of the scheme, Vaughan Yates enlisted the services of Joseph Paxton, celebrated for his remodelling of the gardens at Chatsworth House, Derbyshire, and an advocate of Edwin Chadwick's

Figure 11 *The original plans for the Princes Park scheme included a large number of substantial villas and townhouses. In the event, only a small number were ever erected. Princes Terrace was the largest of these and it continues to shape the character of the park today.* [DP030902]

national movement to improve public health. The importance of Princes Park, as Paxton's first foray into public park design, has often been overshadowed by his larger, more famous projects of Birkenhead Park (1847) and the Crystal Palace (1851). The semi-private status of the park in its early years also means that it does not qualify as the earliest public park. Nevertheless, as the first of Paxton's projects in the public domain, and therefore an exemplar for every substantial Victorian municipal park that was to follow, Princes Park stands as one of the most significant extant examples of early public park design.

At Princes Park, Paxton proved to be no less ambitious than he was in the private employment of the Duke of Devonshire at Chatsworth. He introduced dramatic features such as a large lake, a serpentine carriage drive and an open meadow uninterrupted by paths or structures, transforming the topography of the land and enabling a new range of activities. He also experimented with different sizes and shapes of walks,

Princes Park, Liverpool

Figure 12 *Liverpool's parks could be as attractive during the winter as they were in the summer months. Then, as now, snow-filled landscapes were particularly popular. Postcard publishers quickly took note and photographs taken during the summer months were doctored to supply the demand for wintry scenes. [Nigel Sharp collection]*

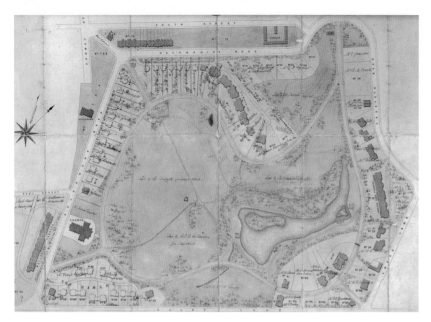

Figure 13 (above) *Early plan of Princes Park. A substantial boating lake, the first to be constructed in a public park in Liverpool, dominates the landscape of Princes Park. [Liverpool Record Office, Liverpool Libraries, Maps and plans]*

Figure 14 (right) *In 1849 a Grand Fancy Fair took place in Princes Park. The event was captured in this lithograph by John Isaac. [Liverpool Record Office, Liverpool Libraries, Binns C.112]*

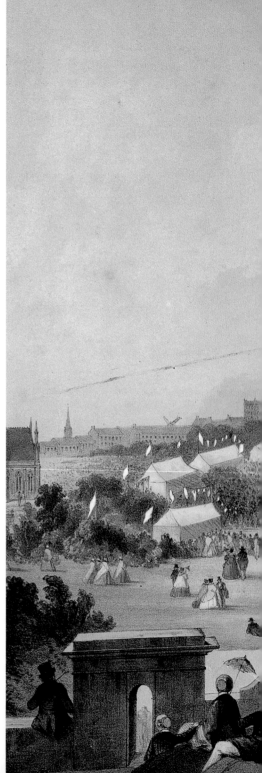

different arrangements of trees and the composition of views (Fig 13). Plans were drawn up from Paxton's instructions by John Robertson, a draftsman to the influential writer and landscape architect of the Derby Arboretum, John Claudius Loudon. Having approved the final plans, Paxton entrusted Edward Milner, his apprentice from the Chatsworth estate, with their realisation.

The architectural and horticultural beauty of the park certainly made it a desirable place to walk and escape the bustle of the city. However, its unprecedented size also created the opportunity to host public events on a far larger scale than had hitherto been attempted. In 1849 it played host to one of the largest events in its history, the 'Philanthropic Festival' or 'Grand Fancy Fair' (Fig 14). Staged to raise money for nearby hospitals, the Grand Fancy Fair was open to all Liverpool's citizens and offered a wide range of amusements and

attractions including a ladies' bazaar for fancy work, a floral and horticultural exhibition, rowing matches, a demonstration of an electric telegraph, a firework display, a camera obscura, ventriloquism and a balloon ascent by the aeronaut Mr Gibbon. Clearly, in addition to the permanent 'passive' attraction of walks and views, Princes Park continued the tradition of urban green space as the location for special public events, where Liverpool's citizens could be entertained by visual spectacles and cultural amusements (Fig 15).

Although sections of the park were reserved for the minority until 1918, public access to the main grounds was celebrated as a great achievement. In 1844 the *Liverpool Mercury* asserted that 'it is delightful to see the labouring man, his wife and children, in the evenings enjoying themselves in the pleasure grounds which have thus, by the munificence of one individual, been set apart, as a place where both the rich and poor may enjoy the refreshing breeze'.[13] Still, the reservation of a small area of the park for exclusive use of wealthy residents prompted criticisms from some observers. Furthermore, the park's main features, its walks, were perceived by some as an out of date and unsatisfactory facility for the city's public. The very elegance of the park's design, its ornamental bridge and locked gardens were considered by many to be a mere extension of a private estate, designed with little consideration for the recreational needs of the wider population (Fig 16). Campaigners for improved standards of public health and a comprehensive plan for green-space provision across Liverpool targeted their criticisms at the Corporation and its initial refusal to co-operate with Vaughan Yates in the creation of a fully public park. Another local newspaper, *The Porcupine*, reminded its readers, that 'Prince's Park – in other words, some prettily laid out walks through private gardens – did not come out of municipal care or generosity'.[14] Although such criticisms continued, in the decades that followed Liverpool was in the forefront of civic provision of urban parks and public gardens. The 'municipal care' of the Corporation of Liverpool was to reach to every corner of the city in the form of a massive scheme of public parks, designed to serve every social strata of the city and quash the criticisms of elitism and exclusivity that had plagued the first generation of 'public' parks.

Figure 15 *Poster advertising the Grand Fancy Fair in Princes Park, 1849. [By courtesy of The University of Liverpool Library]*

Figure 16 *Liverpool's parks became popular tourist destinations throughout the 19th century. Publishers produced numerous souvenir prints to sell to the burgeoning number of visitors. In the days before postcards these images often decorated writing paper or, as in this view of Princes Park's ornamental bridge, by the London firm Rock and Co, were pasted into scrapbooks. [Liverpool Record Office, Liverpool Libraries, Photographs and Small Prints]*

Liverpool's lungs: the creation of the *ribbon of parks*

Despite a large section of Princes Park being open to the public, this new experiment in park creation made little impact upon the well-being of the majority of Liverpool's working-class inhabitants. As it was located on the southern edge of the city, those who lived and worked in the north remained isolated from recreational green space. The adverse effects of this north–south divide were not limited to mere appearances. More importantly for the general prosperity of the city, the divide affected the health of Liverpool's working population.

The city's role as a seaport made it particularly susceptible to outbreaks of contagious diseases, which could arrive in the town via the many ships and cargos that docked at the quayside every day. The threat to public health posed by the city's mercantile character was noted by Dr W S Trench, the Medical Officer for Liverpool. In his 1863 *Report of the Health of Liverpool*, Trench argued that 'the migratory habits of our poor, and the vast stream of people flocking to the banks of the Mersey for pleasure, business, or in transit to other lands, by providing a succession of fresh victims, maintain the constant activity of the contagion'.[15] However, commentators and campaigners such as Edwin Chadwick, who published his famous tract *The Sanitary Condition of the Working Population of Great Britain* in 1842, also identified the physical environment as a crucial factor in the rapid spread of contagious diseases. In the densely built courts and infamous cellar-dwellings of Liverpool, diseases such as typhus and cholera could devastate an entire district. Outbreaks of contagious diseases had recurred throughout the history of the town, but as Liverpool expanded each visitation claimed an ever-greater death toll.

In 1832 and 1846 Liverpool, like much of Britain, was hit by two particularly savage cholera epidemics (Fig 17). Although the disease did not differentiate between the various social classes, the inadequate sanitation and high-density building that characterised many of the poorer districts made them particularly vulnerable to the spread of infection. The Government responded to the latter epidemic with the Public Health Act of 1848, which empowered local authorities to initiate

Tree-lined avenue, Sefton Park.
[DP030918]

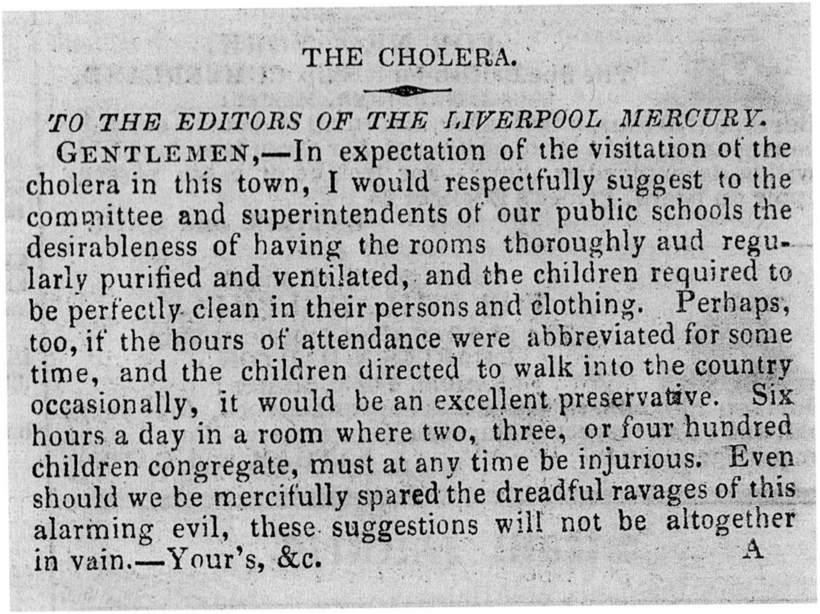

THE CHOLERA.

TO THE EDITORS OF THE LIVERPOOL MERCURY.

GENTLEMEN,—In expectation of the visitation of the cholera in this town, I would respectfully suggest to the committee and superintendents of our public schools the desirableness of having the rooms thoroughly and regularly purified and ventilated, and the children required to be perfectly clean in their persons and clothing. Perhaps, too, if the hours of attendance were abbreviated for some time, and the children directed to walk into the country occasionally, it would be an excellent preservative. Six hours a day in a room where two, three, or four hundred children congregate, must at any time be injurious. Even should we be mercifully spared the dreadful ravages of this alarming evil, these suggestions will not be altogether in vain.—Your's, &c.   A

Figure 17 *The local press continually reported the public health crisis emerging in Liverpool. This letter to the Editor was published in the* Liverpool Mercury, *24 February 1832 and highlights the perceived need for fresh air and ventilation to fend off the disease. [Liverpool Record Office, Liverpool Libraries Hf072 MER]*

sanitary reform projects in their regions and awarded them powers to establish local Boards of Health. Unlike many other cities, Liverpool was swift to utilise its new powers. The main intention of the act was to improve housing, the street infrastructure and sewerage, and the Corporation prohibited the construction of the small enclosed courts which were such a nest of disease and ill health. The act also encouraged environmental improvements, and in this area too the Corporation adopted a radical approach to the city's problems. What resulted was an ambitious and pioneering policy which sought to provide new, extensive green spaces for all its citizens.

In 1850 the Liverpool Improvement Committee advertised for plans for the laying out of unoccupied lands, although not the reintroduction of green space in areas of the city that had already been developed. The result was the proposal to create a *ribbon of parks* around the existing city to give easy access to open space for all its inhabitants. Nevertheless, although the Corporation planned the project, it lacked powers to raise the money necessary for such a large undertaking. Liverpool had to wait 15 years until the Improvement Act of 1865 enabled the Corporation to raise the £500,000 needed to realise the scheme.

A *ribbon of parks*

> If men could only be made without impulses, without passions, without relish for variety, without unconquerable desire for amusement, without a defective physical nature craving for fresh air and out-of-door exercise, and other profane and entirely carnal recreations![16]

The Porcupine's ironic lament, published a decade after the formulation of the plan for the *ribbon of parks*, continued the long-running debate about the health of the city and about the role of public authorities in addressing the problems caused by poor living conditions. By this time the paucity of green spaces in Liverpool, and the deteriorating quality of those which did exist, was openly criticised. Continuing their chastisement of the Corporation, the editors of *The Porcupine* dismissed the Mount Gardens, widely championed nearly a century earlier, as a 'cheerful scrap of blackened grass plot, with all the smoke of the whole line of town and docks agreeably uprising on one side, and the vapours of a charnel-house, the healthful exhalations from our dear brethren and sisters departed, steaming upwards on the other'.[17]

The Porcupine characterised the Corporation of Liverpool's attitude to public park provision as passive and measly, but, in the Corporation's defence, its power to establish and manage public parks and gardens was limited by Parliament. Although empowered to create parks and walks, Corporations were prevented from raising the necessary finances to fund large-scale projects. The Improvement Act, passed by Parliament in 1865, released town Corporations from these restrictions, and to Liverpool's credit the following two decades witnessed a transformation in the authorities' attitude to public green space and its use. The result was a considerable achievement: large-scale provision of open space and the rewriting of the philosophies that underpinned public access and use of

Figure 18 *By the late 19th century, Liverpool offered residents and tourists an array of gardens, parks and playgrounds. [Nigel Sharp collection]*

such sites (Fig 18). The earlier plan, first developed in the 1850s, to create a number of parks on the city's perimeter was revived and became the centrepiece of policy over the next decades.

The *ribbon of parks* scheme was based on the creation of three large parks, one in the north, one in the east and one in the south of the city. The new open spaces were designed to serve all strata of society and improve the health and living standards of the entire urban population. The plan was carried out, by a stupendous effort on the part of public authorities and private speculators, between 1868 and 1872. Although none of the parks – Newsham (opened officially in 1868), Stanley (1870) and Sefton (1872) – entirely realised the hopes of those who invested in them, this was of secondary importance for the majority of Liverpool's population; for them, the parks represented true right of access to open space. Although certain amusements required a small fee, entrance to these municipal parks was free to all. Thus, unlike their predecessors at Ranelagh and Princes Park, Newsham, Sefton and Stanley were established and designed specifically for public recreation. As an account of the opening of Stanley Park argued, 'the park is for the people – the people should use it without let or hindrance; and the only conditions imposed on those who enter should be propriety of behaviour … . The beggar and the prince should be free to use it on this condition.'[18] Still, equality of access did not necessarily result in equal investment and the manner in which the sites were regulated and maintained differed from park to park.

Newsham Park

The first of the great parks to be officially opened to the public was Newsham Park (1868), located to the east of the city centre and laid out on lands previously owned by the Molyneaux family (Fig 19). The Corporation of Liverpool acquired 240 acres of that family's estate as

Figure 19 *The coppice by the lake in Newsham Park provides a naturalistic screen, concealing the boundaries of the park and so creating the illusion of an extensive rural landscape. [DP026181]*

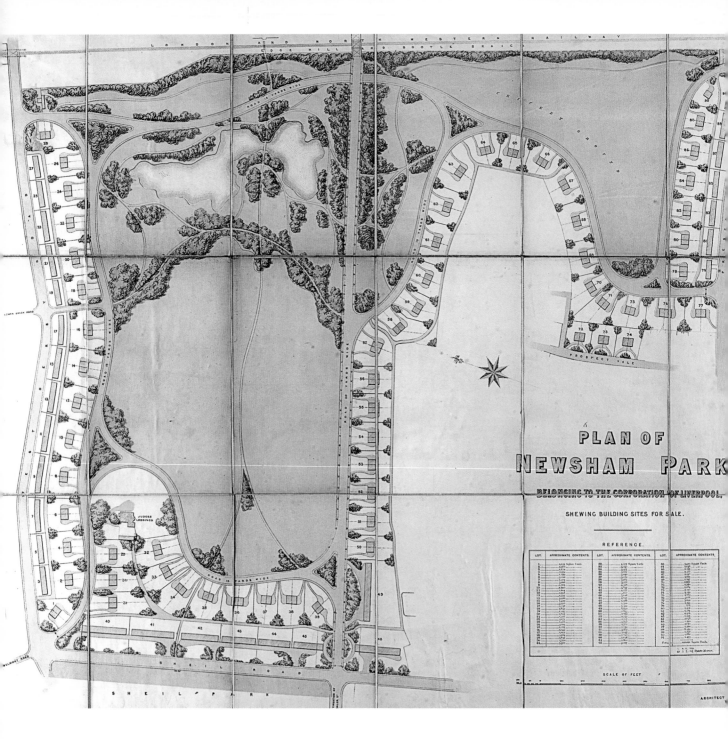

PLAN OF
NEWSHAM PARK

BELONGING TO THE CORPORATION OF LIVERPOOL.

SHEWING BUILDING SITES FOR SALE.

REFERENCE.

SCALE OF FEET

Figure 20 *In a system replicated later at Sefton Park, the area surrounding Newsham Park was divided into land parcels and auctioned off to individual speculators. [Liverpool Record Office, Liverpool Libraries, Maps and Plans]*

early as 1846 with the intention of opening a public park, but a number of obstacles prevented the site from being developed immediately. As with the private enterprise of Princes Park, the construction costs of the park at Newsham were to be subsidised by the sale and lease of neighbouring land to speculative builders. Each plot was then to be developed with a small number of large, detached, residential villas in the mode of earlier prestigious parks such as Regent's Park in London and Birkenhead Park across the Mersey. The designer of the park was Edward Kemp, another of Joseph Paxton's Chatsworth protégés and the superintendent of the pioneering Birkenhead Park. Kemp was well known within middle-class households as the author of the popular treatise *How to Lay Out a Small Garden* (1850) and was one of the judges who had decided the outcome of the significant Central Park design completion in New York (1858). His credentials were formidable but, unfortunately for Kemp and for the ambitions of the Corporation, the middle decades of the 19th century were years of economic instability in Liverpool. The fluctuations in the local economy led to stagnation in the building market and consequently a fall in the value of the land surrounding the proposed park. In addition, the ongoing problem of poor public health and repeated epidemics prompted the site to be recommended as a potential location for a new city cemetery. Although the cemetery proposal was finally rejected, in 1863 the Corporation sold a large piece of land that had been severed from the park by the new Bootle railway line. As a result of these delays and land sales, it was not until 1864 that Edward Kemp's first design for the reduced park was accepted (Fig 20).

Although inhibited by increasing budgetary pressures, Kemp's design for Newsham incorporated a number of substantial features that collectively transformed the plot into a diverse and cultivated landscape. The design effectively divided the park into three main sections: an intensively cultivated area around a lake and a boating pond; a large swathe of open land in front of Newsham House; and a third, annexed area, which received little investment in the initial phase of development. The most ambitious of these areas in terms of construction and cultivation was the large lake and adjacent boating pond, two features which continue to define the park and its use today. Situated in one corner of the park, alongside the road that would become known as Orphanage Drive, the lake was designed along the naturalistic principles favoured by Joseph Paxton and those 18th-century masters of landscape design Humphry Repton and Capability Brown (Fig 21). Although consciously and painstakingly drafted and redrafted, the shape of the lake was intended to appear as natural as the landscape that still survived beyond the boundaries of Britain's expanding cities. To accentuate further the picturesque effect, serpentine paths were incorporated to weave between coppices of trees. These in turn were designed to imitate native woodlands, while a small, inaccessible island on the lake was 'developed' into a miniature wilderness.

In contrast to this decorative section of the park, a large proportion

Figure 21 *The lake, Newsham Park. Created along the same principles as the lake at Princes Park, the lake at Newsham Park is today popular with anglers. [DP026182]*

of the Newsham site was to be relatively sparsely cultivated. Broad areas of lawn, punctuated with occasional coppices of trees and dissected by pathways, were laid out to encourage the healthy pursuit of strolling. A number of these paths followed broadly the routes previously intended for residential avenues and their carriageways. Consequently they cut across the park rather than following the undulating, irregular routes laid out in the picturesque quarter. This open land provided visitors and residents of Newsham and Gardner's Drives with wide and pleasing prospects and would in the following decades become an important venue for more active recreation and, in the annexed quarter, the location of a bandstand. Yet, despite the completion of substantial components of Kemp's design, a number of smaller, decorative features were sacrificed to the diminishing budget.

Laying-out work began at Newsham in 1865 but the plan for integrated housing and parkland continued to struggle throughout the period of its construction. A series of unsuccessful land auctions had left a dire shortfall in the funds required to landscape and embellish the park. In the end, the grandest building on the park perimeter was the Seamen's Orphanage (1871–5), an exercise in philanthropy rather than a commercial triumph and perhaps not helpful in attracting wealthy residents to the area (Fig 22). In 1878, nine years after the first land auction, the aspirations for the residential development around Newsham Park were finally lowered. Plans were drawn up to permit the construction of up to four houses on plots of land previously reserved for a single prestigious detached dwelling. Building speculators responded to this relaxation in the planning restrictions, but many of the plots allocated for housing remained undeveloped, including a large area previously designated for a grand house-lined thoroughfare. Although the 1860s was a decade of continued suburbanisation away from the dense housing of the city centre, Newsham suffered from its remoteness from the fashionable south of the city and failed to attract large numbers of wealthy residents.

The layout and buildings that define Newsham Park today have evolved over the past 150 years. Even features that may appear 'original' and were constructed in the early decades of the park's development were

Figure 22 *The largest and most imposing building to be built on the Newsham site was the Seamen's Orphanage, opened in 1874. Having been used as a hospital in the later 20th century, the building is now empty and vulnerable to vandals and decay.* [DP026179]

not those stipulated by Kemp in his original and revised plans. Some of the park's most famous landmarks – the imposing gates mounted with three-armed lamps that still mark the entrances to the site on Sheil Road, Prescot Road and at the head of Newsham Drive – were not as Kemp had envisaged them (Fig 23). After the completion of the lake and the major landscaping, a lack of funds continued to plague Newsham Park and compromises were made to ensure the completion of the project within the new budget. In 1871 the present gates and lodges were supplied as cheaper alternatives to those included in the original quote and in 1900, over 30 years after works began, four fountains were finally installed in the park, three of which were less expensive than those proposed in Kemp's scheme. Nevertheless, despite their deviation from Kemp's vision, the component parts of Newsham Park combined to produce a relatively coherent and practical public space that served the needs of local visitors (Fig 24). Novel features were added, such as a miniature windmill (c1875) and an aviary (1902) (Fig 25), that provided attractions for residents and catered to the changing demands and aspirations of Liverpool's citizens.

Figure 23 (above) *Now local landmarks, the distinctive gateposts at Newsham Park were supplied in 1871 as a cheaper alternative to those proposed in Kemp's original scheme. [DP026176]*

Figure 24 (left) *By the early 20th century, Newsham Park had developed into a mature landscape, with large trees, well-stocked herbaceous borders and flower beds, and walkways for strolling. [Nigel Sharp collection]*

Figure 25 *Aviaries and petting zoos became a fashionable feature of urban parks in the latter decades of the 19th century. This aviary in Newsham Park was introduced in 1902 and appears to have housed exotic parrots. [Nigel Sharp collection]*

The Aviary, Newsham Park, Liverpool.

Stanley Park

Opened in 1870 and situated to the north of the city centre in Anfield, Stanley Park was located furthest from the fashionable quarters to the south of the town. When the park was first planned in the 1860s, the future character of the area may not have been apparent. Some large residences had been built there in the preceding decades for wealthier citizens who sought to escape the city centre and take advantage of the views. Still, the area was not destined to match the social character of Sefton Park. By the late 1860s, the proximity of numerous dockyards and industrial premises had established the area's reputation as a primarily lower-middle- and working-class neighbourhood. Consequently, unlike the schemes at Princes and Newsham Parks, the Corporation could not rely upon the sale of grand villas to subsidise the Stanley Park development. Nevertheless, financial constraints and disparity between the emerging social composition of Anfield's community and that of Sefton Park did not initially inhibit the Corporation's ambitions for developing an equally large and richly landscaped site for the residents of this quarter of the city. The Corporation's commitment to the scheme was reflected in their decision to again employ Edward Kemp to lay out the 95 acres of grounds.

The Stanley Park plot was divided into two distinct areas, one primarily ornamental and the other left open for recreation. Towards the west, on high ground, a gently sloping ornamental area was divided into a series of smaller sections, each with a distinct function, including the traditional pastimes of walking and 'taking in' the view that had characterised the city's earliest parks over 140 years previously. Along the top is a formal terrace which, in the early years, was heavily planted with carpet bedding (Fig 26). As well as providing neo-Gothic sandstone pavilions that were conveniently located for refreshments and shelter from inclement weather, the terrace also proved a popular viewing platform for locals and tourists alike. By the end of the 19th century, the attraction of the views to north and west had resulted in the erection of a key, to guide viewers through the many landmarks that could be seen from that site. As Leonard Pattern's guide to the city published in 1902 pointed out, 'this esplanade, with wings to right and left, is tastefully laid out with flower beds, and at the eastern side are seen two iron scroll

The Terrace, Stanley Park, Liverpool

Figure 26 *The terrace at Stanley Park was famed for the large and bold carpet beds, laid out by the park's permanent staff of gardeners. [Nigel Sharp collection]*

Figure 27 *The boating lake, Stanley Park c1900, one of the most popular attractions for adults and children alike. [Nigel Sharp collection]*

telescope stands, the tops of which are engraved with the names of the various points of interest to be seen from this vantage ground'.[19] The view not only provided an entertaining diversion, it also created the illusion that the park was far larger than its true extent, for it drew the eye over the increasingly developed neighbourhood towards the surrounding agricultural hinterland. This illusion was further enhanced by the location of Anfield Cemetery immediately beyond the park boundary.

In 1870 the value of this borrowed landscape was recommended to the readers of *The Porcupine*, who were informed that 'the view here is magnificent; and we can hardly say where the park ends, as it appears to be part of the open country, vast in size, rich in wooded embellishments, and picturesque to a high degree'.[20] However, the impact of the view may have been hampered by local industries, as the *Illustrated London News* reported that it was 'commonly obscured by the smoke of the factory districts'.[21] Below the formal terrace gardens, Kemp's original design incorporated a middle ground of soft, informal landscaping, which complemented the distant natural landscape, beyond which was a more structured series of walks and lakes at the northern extreme of the park. Over the following half-century, this 'picturesque' area was to house the majority of the park's attractions, including an aviary, a children's dell, a swimming pool and a series of ornamental bridges, but at the time of the park's official opening in May 1870 it was reserved for promenading and boating (Fig 27).

The other half of the park was left largely undeveloped and was consequently adopted as a site for sports, both organised and informal. It was in this area that Everton football club played its earliest matches, before relocating to the Anfield site in 1884. Prohibited in Sefton Park, football and other contact sports were encouraged in Stanley Park as healthy pursuits for the working classes of the area. Children's sports days and fetes were common in the early years of the park, enabled by the large and distinct stretch of open space. Yet, although it clearly proved a popular resort for locals and tourists alike, the large scale of Stanley Park, both in terms of geographical area and financial investment, did not quash criticisms of a north–south divide in park provision. Observers perceived discrepancies between the quality of landscaping and maintenance of Sefton Park and its sister parks at Stanley and Newsham. In 1879 a correspondent for the *Liberal Review* highlighted the disparity:

> Sefton Park is situated far from the centre of the population. Those who most need a park reside at least four or five miles away from it. The parks at Stanley are more accessible, and are more calculated to be of real benefit to the mass of the population – to those, in fact, who pay the rates. Aristocratic Liverpool has not, however, condescended to adopt them as places of residence. Therefore we do not find that the Improvement Committee are as extravagant in their demands in relation to them as they are in regard to Sefton Park.[22]

Sefton Park

Notwithstanding the value placed upon Stanley Park by residents and visitors, and the contribution that it made to the realisation of the *ribbon of parks* across Liverpool, it was a different location that, from its commencement, represented a substantial triumph for the city and a trophy for advocates of the parks movement. Sefton Park, situated close to Princes Park on the wealthy southern perimeter of the city, was the most elaborately landscaped and embellished of all the new park sites (Fig 28). The apparent favouritism exercised towards this site by

Figure 28 *Evergreen coppice, Sefton Park. The city's parks are planted with a diverse range of trees and shrubs. This coppice of evergreen trees near the Palm House ensures there is shade and colour all year round.* [DP030922]

Figure 29 *Facilities for public benefit were woven into the design of many Victorian metropolitan parks. This neo-Gothic drinking fountain in Sefton Park was situated close to the boathouse, on one of the main walking routes around the lake. [DP030933]*

Liverpool's civic leaders was doubtless driven by the belief that it would consolidate the superior character of the area. As with Newsham and Stanley Parks, a piece of land was initially purchased by the Corporation, prior to the confirmation of any fixed design for the site. However, unlike these other developments, the design of the park was decided in a public competition, with a prize of 300 guineas for the winning scheme. Despite the site's remit as a public space, the brief was remarkably similar to that of the nearby Princes Park. In addition to the 160 acres of building plots necessary to assist in funding the project, the brief specified a private garden for the residents of the villas. Although never actually realised, this intention to retain a portion of Sefton Park for private use suggests that expectations surrounding accessibility differed in relation to the perceived social and economic status of a neighbourhood. Such ideological distinctions were necessarily reflected in the physical design of the parks.

In May 1867 the chosen design was announced as the combined work of Edouard André, Gardener in Chief to the city of Paris, and Lewis Hornblower, a Liverpool architect. André was to be responsible for the general layout and landscaping, while Hornblower attended to the buildings within the park. Both designers had extensive experience of ornamental landscapes. Seven years earlier, André had been appointed *Jardinier Principal* (Head Gardener) for the city of Paris, while local boy Hornblower had designed the grand entrance for Birkenhead Park and had worked on the designs for the lodges and gates at nearby Princes Park. The prize-winning plan included a wealth of features ranging from a review ground, an archery lawn, a 'rotton row' for recreational horse riding, a deer park, a botanic garden, a lake and a Moorish pavilion to an ornamental windmill, an aviary and a number of optional 'ornamental accessories' including a grotto, Gothic fountain and rock tunnel (Fig 29). Clearly, the patronage anticipated for Sefton Park differed considerably from that expected for Stanley and Newsham Parks. This 'superior' character was emphasised by the largely successful, if slow, development of the perimeter lands as substantial villa residences – an achievement not duplicated at either of the other sites.

The grandeur of Sefton Park was ensured from the earliest stages of its construction. Compromises were made during its laying out and

continued throughout the decades that followed, but its location in the socially exalted territory of south Liverpool ensured that the ambitions of its architects were respected and encouraged where possible. Although not all planned features were realised at Sefton Park, many of them were constructed during the 1870s and further embellishments added over the following decades. Aside from the formal, architectural components of the park, André and Hornblower paid great attention to the horticultural content and the manner in which it contributed to the experience of the site. In contrast to Kemp's design at Newsham, there were to be no serpentine or wholly straight paths as they were felt to be ill-suited to the natural topography of the area. Instead, the architects responded to the existing landscape and sought to enhance the natural beauty with well-considered planting. André introduced sweeping curves in the style favoured by his Parisian colleague Jean Charles Adolphe Alphand, while the colour of foliage, as well as the location of trees, was used to enhance the illusion of distance between coppices and create the sense that the viewer was within a park of a far greater extent than could be achieved in such an urban area (Fig 30). Enclosed areas, such as the dell, provided an environmental contrast to the grand prospects enjoyed in much of the park, but nevertheless, the scale of these confined and densely cultivated areas and their sophisticated planting reflected a similar level of ambition and commitment to the site's long-term maintenance (Fig 31).

Figure 30 (above) *Foliage, Sefton Park. Even during the colder months, the parks still have a lot to offer. The colourful display of autumn leaves at Sefton Park attracts visitors from near and far. [DP030936]*

Figure 31 (right) *The dell was one of Sefton Park's main attractions. Incorporating the brook and a rockery, it was also the original location for the Peter Pan statue, now situated outside the Palm House. [DP026234]*

Figure 32 (left) *The main gates, Sefton Park. The numerous gates, screens and lodge houses that surround Sefton Park were constructed over a five-year period. The area around the main gates, constructed in the Gothic style, was finally completed in 1875, three years after the park was officially opened. [DP030896]*

Figure 33 (below) *The rock tunnel, adjacent to the boating lake, Sefton Park. [DP026188]*

Applauded by the city's worthies, the grandeur of the design did not meet with universal approval. For some, the elaborate features and extensive relandscaping of the land was cause for regret. As the local resident A G Kurtz observed in his diary entry for 19 December 1871:

> I took a walk through Sefton Park which they seem to be making head with. Spite of everything its beauties look very tame, its waters like canals & its rocks & cascades very artificial. As the trees grow, of course, it will improve, but for a Park I think the style of laying it out is small & more like landscape gardening than park scenery.[23]

Notwithstanding Kurtz's complaints, on the day that it opened Sefton Park presented a grand effect to visitors. It was originally enclosed by high iron railings, limiting access and channelling visitors through large monumental gateways. The Gothic gates (1875), screen (1870), and lodges (1870 and 1874) at Sefton were some of the last structures to be completed in the initial phase of construction (Fig 32). The architectural model chosen for them reflected the mid-Victorian enthusiasm for neo-Gothic, a style inspired by the ancient Gothic architecture of western Europe and the variety and irregularity displayed by nature. Appropriately for a park, many neo-Gothic motifs were commonly appropriated from leaves, vines, fruits and blossoms. The designs for the lodges were provided by the Borough Surveyor, Thomas Shelmerdine, rather than Lewis Hornblower, but their Gothic character complemented the site's many naturalistic features such as the cascade, rock tunnel and grotto (Fig 33). At Sefton the effect was dramatic, and testified to the value placed upon the design and construction of the buildings. However, in addition to championing the status of the park as a fashionable place of resort, these entrances, and their extravagant displays of ironwork and stonework, communicated more implicit messages to those who spent their time within the park boundaries. Although ostensibly 'public', Sefton Park and the other municipal parks in the scheme were not 'open' or unregulated landscapes. The reputation of parks as safe havens was essential to attract respectable visitors, and efforts were made to control access and deter the disreputable. In a similar manner to the garden squares created decades earlier, the new municipal parks of Liverpool were locked and policed at night. Therefore, park gates and their adjacent lodges were symbols of regulation and supervision but they also contributed to the safety of the park in a practical way. Park lodges were frequently inhabited by park keepers and gardeners who provided a security presence at park entrances, day and night.

These measures did not, however, eliminate abuses, and it appears to have been relatively easy to thwart the security measures put in place by the Corporation and exercised by the park keepers. Initial fears that Sefton Park would remain the preserve of the wealthy few were slowly supplanted by concerns about its 'inappropriate' use, especially after dark (Figs 34 and 35). In contrast to their advertised purpose as a means of improving the health and moral welfare of the city, parks could be associated with morally dubious behaviour, as local newspaper *The Liverpool Citizen* argued:

> We have heard a great deal recently about social purity, and the rest of it. What do the Parks' Committee say to the condition of Sefton Park after dark? The few keepers are useless. The plain truth had better be said publicly. The condition of the park after dark is a scandal and a disgrace to the city and Corporation of Liverpool. A number of servant girls, shop girls, and nondescript young wanderers are enticed into the place for the lowest motives …. At present it is a hot-bed of iniquity instead of a healthy breathing place for the community.[24]

Despite the obvious ambition in André and Hornblower's vision, the realisation of their design repeatedly fell short of expectations. Although it was eventually developed around its entire periphery, the sale of building plots and the completion of works at Sefton did not proceed at the rate originally anticipated. By 1872, the year that the park was officially opened by Prince Arthur, a number of features had already been eliminated from the plan. These included over 70 villas (the majority within the park grounds) and the archery and cricket ground (Fig 36). However, new additions were also made, including new footpaths, the iron bridge (1873) and the distinctive Palm House (Fig 37), donated by

Figure 34 (top left) *Despite being situated in a smart residential area, Sefton Park acquired the reputation as a place for nocturnal assignations between domestic servants from the nearby villas. [Nigel Sharp collection]*

Figure 35 (bottom left) *The city's parks appeared in a number of novelty postcards that combined images of their famous landmarks with cheeky mottos and illustrations. [Nigel Sharp collection]*

Figure 36 (below) *Cricket was one of the earliest sports to be permitted in Sefton Park. Sefton Park Cricket Club continues this long tradition. [DP026250]*

Henry Yates Thompson in 1896 along with six statues: three celebrating Liverpool's maritime pride and three commemorating major contributors to botanic science and gardening. As with earlier parks and walks in Liverpool, Sefton Park continued to evolve to serve the changing requirements and economic fortunes of the city's inhabitants and the perception of the park by locals and visitors alike also altered over time.

Notwithstanding concerns regarding social propriety and fluctuations in the economic fortunes of the city, Sefton remained the most prestigious site in Liverpool's *ribbon of parks*. However, the original intention to erect private residences and allot private gardens represented very limited progress in the provision of a truly public park for the city. It was Stanley Park, designed to serve the inhabitants of north Liverpool, which realised this ambition most authentically.

Figure 37 (left) *Restored and reopened in 2001, the Palm House at Sefton Park has become one of the city's most famous landmarks. [DP030945]*

Servicing the parks: public facilities and park maintenance

The mere provision of a park was not universally recognised as the fulfilment of the Corporation's responsibilities, nor was it considered to be so by the Corporation itself. Maintenance, development, improvement, and an equal commitment to these requirements in every park were perceived to be just as important as the initial investment in land. Even before the parks were completed, maintenance sheds and other ancillary buildings were constructed to house park keepers' equipment and to secure assets, such as leisure boats, during the winter. In some instances designs for these buildings were included in the original architects' plans. Boathouses, in particular, were recognised as an essential attendant feature of any substantial stretch of water and those at both Princes and Sefton Parks were completed in the first phases of their development. Although both have been unfortunately lost to arson in recent years, they were two of the most

Figure 38 *Notwithstanding the numerous regulations that governed behaviour in Sefton Park, it remained a place for fun and relaxation. The area around the boating lake was often crowded during the summer months. [Liverpool Record Office, Liverpool Libraries, Photographs and Small Prints]*

Figure 39 *The striking mock-Tudor boathouse at Sefton Park has unfortunately been lost to arson in recent years.*

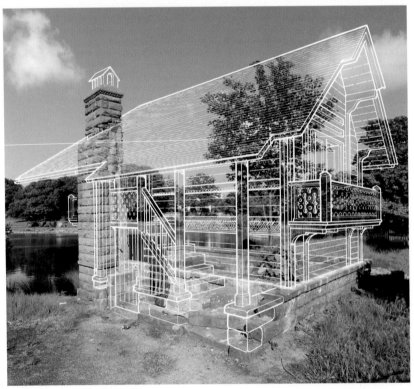

Figure 40 *The boathouse at Princes Park: the chimney that heated the upper floor is the only original feature that survives above the footings.*

TUESDAY, JUNE 11th.

By kind permission of Colonel the Hon. Heneage Legge and Officers of the Regiment.

BAND OF THE 9th (QUEEN'S ROYAL) LANCERS

(Hulme Barracks, Manchester).

Conductor .... Mr. William Winter.

AFTERNOON.

1—March.. 'Hoch Habsburg' .... Kral
2—Overture.. 'Crown Diamonds' .... Auber
3—Valse.. 'Pastoral Songs' .... Bucquoit
4—Selection .. 'La vie Parisienne' .... Offenbach
5—Cornet Polka.. 'The Village Festival '.. Clement
      Cornet Soloist...Corporal O. Knight.
6—Polonaise.. 'Lebewohl ' .... Gordecke
7—Fantasia.. 'A Burlesque' .... Kappey
      (On old and humorous melodies).
8—Valse.. 'Daddy' .... Bucalossi
      ' God save the Queen.'

EVENING.

1— 'Danse des Paysans Russes' .... Ascher
2—Overture.. 'The Bohemian Girl' .... Balfe
3—Aria Conversazioni.'Diamants de la Couronne' Auber
      Clarionet Soloist.... Corporal A. Murdoch.
4—Selection .. 'Maritana' .... Wallace
5—Valse.. .... Waldteufel
6—Divertissement ...'Vervandle Seelen' ... Eilenberg
      (Kindred Minds).
      Two Cornets Soli....Corporal O. Knight
      and Private Davidson.
7—Selection .. 'Indigo' .... Chassaigne
8—Galop.. 'Violet' .... Lamont
      ' God save the Queen.'

By kind permission of Captain Groom,

BAND OF THE LIVERPOOL TRAINING SHIP "INDEFATIGABLE."

AFTERNOON.

1—March .. 'St. Cecilia' .... Kottaun
2—Valse.. 'Daisy' .... Rimsdorff
3—Polka.. 'Black and Tan' .... C. Lonthian
4—Selection .. 'The Sorcerer' .... Sullivan
5—Air and Chorus.. 'Gathering Shells by the Sea' Thompson
6—Valse.. 'Swinging .... Ed. Silva
7—Schottische.. 'Golden Crown' .... A. B. Smith
8—Lancers .. 'H.M.S. Pinafore' .... Sullivan
9—Valse.. 'Dorothy' .... Cellier
10—Descriptive Polka.. 'A Sleigh Ride' ... Jullien

EVENING.

1—March .. 'Indefatigable' .... A. B. Smith
2—Overture .. 'Marionettes' .... C. Gurlitt
3—Gavotte.. 'Stephanie' .... Czibulki
4—Valse.. 'Estudiantina' .... Waldteufel
5—Selection.. 'Dorothy' .... Cellier
6—Air and Chorus 'Away to the Mountain's Brow' A. Lee
7—Valse.. 'Bon Voyage' .... Carl Malmsberg
8—Schottische.. 'La Grande Inn' .... Lamotte
9—Quadrille.. 'Mantouax Noirs' .... Bucalossi
10—Fantasia 'The Smithy in the Wood' .. Michaelis
      ' Rule Britannia' and ' God save the Queen.'

By kind permission of the Rev. Canon Lester,

BAND OF THE KIRKDALE CERTIFIED INDUSTRIAL SCHOOLS.

WEDNESDAY, JUNE 12th.

By kind permission of Colonel Lord Downe and Officers of the Regiment.

BAND OF THE 10th ROYAL HUSSARS (York).

Conductor .... Mr. A. Williams.

AFTERNOON.

1—'War March of Priests' (from Athalie) Mendelssohn
2—Overture.. 'Massaniello ' .... Auber
3—Valse.. 'Pluie d'Or' .... Waldteufel
4—Selection 'Carmen' .... Bizet
5—Song .. 'The Better Land ' .... Cowen
6—Overture.. 'Zampa ' .... Herold
7—'Birthday Serenade' .... Rivoldt
8—Selection.. 'The Yeomen of the Guard' Sullivan
9—Valse.. 'Venus Reigen ' .... Gung'l
10—Polka.. 'L'Esprit Francais' .... Waldteufel

EVENING.

1—'Marche aux Flambeaux' .... Meyerbeer
2—Overture 'William Tell' .... Rossini
3—Valse.. 'Journalisten' .... Strauss
4—Selection. 'Faust' .... Gounod
5—Bolero.. Io son la ross' .... Kariani
6—Song.. 'The Lost Chord' .... Sullivan
7—Selection .. 'Falka ' .... Chassaigne
8—Valse.. 'Golden Leaves' .... A. B. Smith
9—Polka.. 'Wooden Shoes' .... Oscar Seydel
10—Descriptive Fantasia, 'A Hunting Scene, Bucalossi

By kind permission of Captain Groome,

BAND OF THE TRAINING SHIP "INDEFATIGABLE."

AFTERNOON.

1—March .. 'William Tell' .... Rossini
2—Selection.. 'Patience' .... Sullivan
3—Valse.. ' My Queen' .... Bucalossi
4—Gavotte.. 'Heimlichen Liebe' .... Resch
5 Cavatina.. 'Torquato Tasso' .... Donizetti
6—Quadrille.. 'Les Cloches de Corneville,' Planquette
7—Selection .. 'Trovatore ' .... Verdi
8—Valse.. 'Golden Leaves' .... A. B. Smith
9—Polka.. 'Trovatore' .... Verdi
10—Descriptive Polka..'A Hunting Scene,' Bucalossi

EVENING.

1—'Marcia Fantastique ' .... A. B. Smith
2—Selection.. 'Cornflower' .... C. Coote
3—Lancers 'Pirates of Penzance' .... Sullivan
4—Selection.. 'Olivette ' .... Audran
5—Air and Chorus.'The Assassination of Mr.
      C. Robin' .... Ed. Forman
6—Valse.. 'Nell Gwynne' .... Planquette
7—Polka.. 'Katschke' .... Stamy
8—Danse Romanesca (Italian Dance) .... Massot
9—Valse.. 'Royal Route ' .... Ed. Annes
10—Descriptive Galop..'The Express Train, Wahlbrenner
      'Rule Britannia' and ' God save the Queen.'

By kind permission of the Rev. Canon Lester,

BAND OF THE KIRKDALE CERTIFIED INDUSTRIAL SCHOOLS.

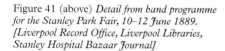

Liverpool.

Newsham Park, Ea...

Wrench Series, No. 4402.

your sincere friend Lizzie

Figure 41 (above) *Detail from band programme for the Stanley Park Fair, 10–12 June 1889. [Liverpool Record Office, Liverpool Libraries, Stanley Hospital Bazaar Journal]*

Figure 42 (above, right) *The elaborate cast-iron bandstand in Newsham Park was originally surrounded by decorative bedding plants, providing an attractive focal point in the eastern quarter of the park. [Nigel Sharp collection]*

substantial structures within Liverpool's parks in the latter decades of the 19th century (Figs 38, 39 and 40).

Later additions to parks varied in character and purpose. Some were essentially decorative, with the miniature windmill erected in Newsham Park in *c*1875 and the three fountains introduced to the lower terrace at Stanley Park in the early 1900s serving to amuse and delight the strolling families. Alternatively, new features might provide additional entertainment for visitors. In Stanley Park the demand for musical performances, established in the pleasure gardens of the 18th century, was met by the introduction of a bandstand in 1899, and bands were hired to perform at each of the parks at different times throughout the summer season (Figs 41 and 42). Alongside these conspicuous buildings were a host of modest booths, kiosks and huts, each providing a distinct service to the emerging park 'consumer'. Across Britain, ice-cream stands, cafés and even public toilets within parks were licensed by local authorities but leased by private individuals or companies. As a result of this semi-privatised service industry within parks, the structures that housed such facilities were often temporary and wholly functional.

Some, such as the carts and ice-cream wagons that served a seasonal business, were entirely absent from the park landscape during winter months. Unlike the more substantial boathouses and glasshouses, few such features were incorporated into original park designs and with no extant examples one can only speculate as to how many such buildings were erected and demolished in the early decades of Liverpool's metropolitan parks. Nevertheless, however small their scale and perfunctory their architecture, these modest structures performed an important and central role in shaping the park experience for many of Liverpool's 19th- and early 20th-century inhabitants.

Contrasting with the buildings designed for public use was a hidden world, intentionally concealed from visitors. The planting schemes in the parks demanded cultivation of huge numbers of plants in specially created nurseries. These horticultural installations were often set to one side in the parks: at Sefton, there was an extensive nursery, with outbuildings and glasshouses on Ibbotson's Lane, and at Newsham and Stanley there were similar yards beside the lodges at one of the main entrances. The plants grown in these busy working areas were used not just for the parks themselves, but also for civic occasions; it was said of the Botanic Garden, for example, that it 'cost seventeen hundred a year, a great deal of which goes in gardeners' wages, growing flowers for Town Hall banquets, balls, &c., &c, to the great edification of a favoured few sycophants and parasites of the Corporation'.[25] At Calderstones Park, acquired by the Corporation in 1902, the potting sheds that had served the kitchen gardens of a wealthy Merseyside family were put to use serving the changing demands of a new, modern park infrastructure (Figs 43 and 44).

Although frequented by thousands of visitors every year, two of the most famous landmarks of the city's parks – the Palm House at Sefton Park (1896) and the Gladstone Conservatory in Stanley Park (1900) (Fig 45) – also contained secret chambers, rarely accessed by the public. These glass palaces, both gifts to the city by Henry Yates Thompson, brought with them the need for substantial furnaces to maintain the high temperatures required for the tropical plants displayed in the hothouses (Fig 46). Rather than building additional sheds above ground, as had

Figures 43 and 44 *The potting sheds at Calderstones Park continue to be used for their intended purpose. [DP031283, DP031284]*

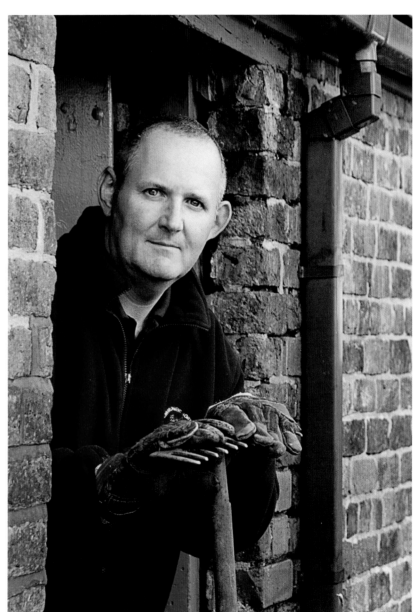

Gladstone Conservatory, Stanley Park, LIVERPOOL.

Figure 45 *Along with the Palm House at Sefton Park, the Gladstone Conservatory at Stanley Park was donated by the city elder Henry Yates Thompson in 1900. [Nigel Sharp collection]*

been common practice in private estate gardens, in both instances the works were located in large basement chambers directly below the elegant glass structures. By utilising underground space in this way, the main body of the glasshouses was left clear of machinery, enabling the cultivation of large and impressive botanical specimens. Beyond the practical advantages of this system, the concealment of the heating system added to the mystery and excitement of the hothouses, where visitors could enjoy tropical temperatures on wet winter afternoons.

Over a period of only two decades the character and extent of Liverpool's parks had been transformed. From a city that threatened to engulf every green space in a never-ending land grab, Liverpool had set the international standard in public park provision. By employing some of the world's most influential and ground-breaking landscape architects, the Corporation had ensured a legacy of accessible green space and historically significant structures, views and facilities. Notwithstanding the funding problems faced at Newsham Park and the many compromises made at each of the sites, the principle of providing extensive municipal parks within highly urbanised commercial and industrial cities was firmly established in Liverpool and held up as an inspiration to other, less progressive, local authorities. Yet Liverpool's parks did not remain inert and unchanged in the decades following their

Figure 46 *Cross-section of a 19th-century glasshouse furnace. [From Hazard's brochure for* Heating Apparatus for Warming and Ventilating Public and Private Buildings *(Bristol 1844), © The British Library Board. All Rights Reserved 1609/2749 p11]*

Figure 47 *The decorative knot beds at Wavertree Botanic Garden were a popular attraction of that site and reflected the grand historical tradition of the British knot garden. Although neglected and overgrown, their general design has survived and can still be made out today.* [DP031048]

'completion'. Features were added and removed to serve the needs of the parks' patrons and the changing priorities of the Corporation (Fig 47). With these changes and improvements came new challenges as the arrival of new parks led to older, traditional facilities suffering relative neglect, and by 1888, the decline of the Botanic Garden was evident:

> This wretched vegetable mausoleum hasn't the claim for a moment's consideration. It's only source of revenue through all last year is specially given in the Corporate accounts as follows 'One Dead horse … £1 5s. 0d.' Whether the horse lost its way on the gardens, and died of starvation for lack of herbage, or whether it committed suicide, overcome by the prevailing melancholy of the surroundings, I don't know. Everything seems to die in the 'gardens,' whether trees, or bulbs, or cuttings. I would sooner die than live there. That horse was not wrong.[26]

Maintenance costs, fluctuating visitor numbers, athletic trends and the economic pressures of commercial development quickly emerged as ongoing features of park management, and each of these factors was to challenge and shape Liverpool's green spaces throughout the 20th century.

CHAPTER 3

Recreation and war

By the early 20th century, Liverpool's *ribbon of parks*, originally located on the outskirts of the city, had become engulfed by suburbia and embedded in the wider urban infrastructure. While they continued to be patronised for the traditional Sunday excursions and pleasure trips, their position between the commercial centre of Liverpool and outlying suburbs made them useful access routes between the two. The paths and internal carriage ways that had been designed to serve the wealthy inhabitants of the parks' villas provided a more pleasant route into the city than main roads and railways. Similarly, the smaller city-centre squares and open spaces such as St John's Gardens became lunchtime retreats for white collar workers (Fig 48). As a result of their continued and varied functions, Liverpool's parks and gardens were celebrated for their usefulness to every sector of society. In his official handbook to Liverpool's parks, Michael O'Mahony described the parks as places where 'youth is served on tennis court, cricket field, boating lake and

Figure 48 (right) *Laid out by Thomas Shelmerdine in 1904, St John's Gardens are one the most substantial green spaces in the historic city centre and complemented the function of the large public parks in Liverpool's suburbs. [DP026272]*

(left) *Giant draughts in Princes Park, 1943. [Liverpool Record Office, Liverpool Libraries, Photographs and Small Prints]*

gymnasium; where boisterous boyhood feels at home; where age can find tranquillity in the Rest Garden and quiet retreat; where infancy is lured by the paddling pool' (Fig 49).[27]

The 19th century had produced a legacy of high-quality and extensive green space in Liverpool but the city's acquisition of public parks did not cease at the close of that century. The 20th century witnessed a massive increase in the Corporation's parks estate, but one that depended more upon the city's good fortune than strategic planning. As the city expanded beyond its 19th-century limits, there was certainly a perceived need for additional green space in the developing outer suburbs, and this was provided principally by the donation or purchase of country house estates. Bought in 1902, the 94-acre Calderstones Park,

Figure 49 *The boathouse and lake, Stanley Park, c1900. The area around the boating lake was once occupied by a number of small huts from which visitors could hire a boat or purchase food and drink. They were insubstantial in their construction and so, unfortunately, none survives. [Nigel Sharp collection]*

in the south-east suburbs of the city, was acquired by the Corporation in the same year as the 120-acre Walton Hall Park. Eleven years later, in 1913, Calderstones Park was united with the neighbouring Harthill estate, adding an additional 32½ acres to the Corporation's park portfolio. Many other estates, large and small, followed throughout the century including the immense Croxteth Country Park, which came into council ownership as recently as 1989. Nevertheless, the great show parks of the 19th century remained the main attractions for Liverpool residents and tourists alike. During the 20th century the status and use of these sites changed dramatically as they came under the influence of new forces. Tourism, war and political upheaval would each play their part in the transformation of the city's green spaces, the gradual decline in their use, and the dramatic decline in their condition.

Tourism and sport

> Liverpudlians can congratulate themselves in possessing so many beautiful Parks. The visitor will find it a simple matter to reach any of these delightful spots by taking advantage of the excellent system of electric trams, or by a short railway journey.[28]

In addition to the ongoing use of parks by the city's citizens, there was an interesting reversal of roles between Liverpool and its neighbouring seaside resorts in the early 20th century, when the city's parks were promoted as worthwhile excursion destinations for holidaymakers from New Brighton, Southport and Blackpool (Fig 50). Merseyside's extensive transport links made all the parks easily accessible by foot or tram and special attractions such as the hothouses at Sefton and Stanley proved particularly popular with visitors prior to 1939. However, although traditional events such as concerts and fairs remained firm favourites among visitors and locals, these occasional entertainments were increasingly supplemented by more permanent facilities that were intended to serve the local community on a daily basis and which included playgrounds, tennis courts and swimming pools.

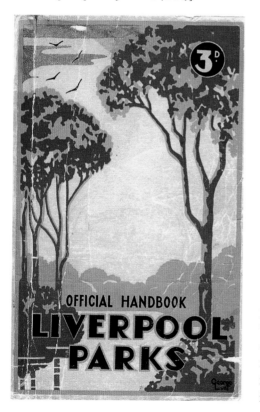

Figure 50 *During the 1930s, Liverpool's parks were promoted in a number of new guide books and brochures. [Liverpool City Council (1934)]*

Following a national trend, the early decades of the century saw an increasing emphasis placed upon sport and active recreation in Liverpool's parks. In 1907 the underused 'rotten row' or bridleway at Stanley Park was symbolically redefined as a 'cycle track', more democratic and accessible, while in the same decade boating was introduced onto the previously ornamental fish pond. By the 1920s, the emphasis upon active, as opposed to traditional 'passive', exercise was so far advanced as to prompt the creation of two swimming pools and a paddling pool (1923), additional bowling greens and a brick club house at Stanley Park (1927 and c1930). This was a move replicated not only across Liverpool, but also across the country as bowling and swimming were recognised to be popular and cheap ways to improve the health of the nation (Figs 51 and 52).

Although sport was universally championed as a benefit to society, the manner in which it was incorporated into existing parks differed from site to site. At Stanley Park, football dominated the agenda, continuing the link forged in 1878 when Everton football club played its first match in the park. Football pitches were introduced at Newsham Park in 1934 to provide an additional attraction for visitors. Yet football was restricted,

BOWLING GREENS, MUIRHEAD GARDENS, WEST DERBY.

Figure 51 *Bowling greens, like this one at West Derby, constituted some of the earliest green spaces in Liverpool. Unlike football and cricket pitches, they could be enjoyed by women as well as by men. [Katy Jones collection]*

Figure 52 *The bowls pavilion, Calderstones Park.*
[DP026147]

if not prohibited, in ornamental parks and in the 'smarter' locations to the south of the city. Here, cricket and tennis emerged as the fashionable pursuits of the upwardly mobile middle classes, and pitches and courts were incorporated into even the smallest of the city's green spaces. In contrast to the large football crowds that were drawn to Stanley Park, cricket and tennis attracted a far smaller, exclusive section of society who wished to emulate the traditional English pastimes of the leisured classes. As one contemporary observer put it, 'you will find at Sefton Park the nearest thing in Liverpool to cricket on the village green'.[29]

Figure 53 (left) *Originally installed in Sefton Park in 1928, Sir George Frampton's bronze statue of Peter Pan has recently been restored. [DP030957]*

Thus, although by the 1930s sport was universally embraced as a fitting feature of public parks, the manner in which facilities were adopted and adapted in different parks served to consolidate existing disparities between the perceived quality and function of the city's green spaces.

The shift towards active recreation and sport was especially noticeable in the increasing provision of facilities for children. As O'Mahony argued, 'If the youth of the City is to grow up into strong and virile men and women, then the necessary playing fields for exercise and recreation must be at their disposal. A sound physique is the best guarantee against disease.'[30] The improvement of public health was clearly a persuasive argument for providing facilities for children. However, there were other implicit and perhaps romantic reasons for investing in playgrounds, dells, statues and paddling pools (Fig 53). In a city comprising densely developed terraced streets and industrial premises, parks provided exotic and fantastic locations for children to pursue imaginative games (Fig 54). The connection between imaginary and real environments was made explicit in a number of attractions introduced in the 1920s. In 1926 a children's garden was created in Stanley Park, decorated with statues inspired by the children's classic

Figure 54 (right) *Children in fancy dress for Liverpool's Royal Day Celebrations, Wavertree Botanic Garden, 1904. [Liverpool Record Office, Liverpool Libraries, from Mowll and Morrison, Visit to Liverpool of Edward VII and Alexandra, Liverpool, 1907]*

Figure 55 *Audley Gardens, Stanley Park, c1929. [Nigel Sharp collection]*

THE PIRATE SHIP IN SEFTON PARK, LIVERPOOL.

Figure 56 *The first of three miniature pirate ships for children, Sefton Park, c1930. [Katy Jones collection]*

Alice in Wonderland (Fig 55). The local newspaper, the *Daily Post and Mercury*, explained in 1931 that 'there is a wishing well in Stanley Park – a part of the paraphernalia of the Children's Garden. It is not, of course, a genuine medieval relic, but an imitation of the shrines of superstitious times, set up in the midst of a modern city to interest the children – young and old.'[31] Sefton Park's response was to erect a statue of Peter Pan and in 1929 to introduce buccaneering adventure in the form of the first of three small-scale pirate ships (Fig 56). The shape, character and content of Liverpool's parks were evolving in response to both the changing needs of the local population and changing ideologies in public space provision.

Figure 57 *Storage huts and bowling pavilions, Stanley Park. Although buildings like these were not part of the original scheme for the park and could intrude upon attractive vistas, they demonstrate the city's response to the changing needs of park users in the 20th century. [DP026282]*

Although to some extent these additions and changes represented a step forward in the provision of park services and facilities, every new feature had the potential to damage the integrity and cohesion of original park designs. Bowling greens required club houses, and swimming pools necessitated the construction of changing rooms, which were essentially temporary structures, erected with little attention to the wider park scheme (Fig 57). The result was that vistas and views, so important to the aesthetic quality of the parks, were increasingly eclipsed by a series of modern buildings built in a variety of styles and materials. Nevertheless, whatever the impact of such structures, no new facility impacted upon the shape, appearance, use and perception of Liverpool's parks to the same extent as did the two periods of international conflict: 1914–18 and 1939–45.

War

The two great wars of the 20th century placed different and sometimes contradictory demands upon Liverpool's public green spaces. During the First World War the impact upon public access to parks was relatively limited as the majority of sites remained open throughout the conflict. However, well-established patterns of use such as sport, recreation and entertainment were joined by new, war-related functions such as food production. Rare photographs of Calderstones Park illustrate the extent of market gardening on that site in July 1917, when American food imports into the Liverpool dockyards were reduced by enemy attacks on shipping (Fig 58). Vegetables as well as cereal crops were grown on the large tracts of land provided by the former estate park, supplying the region, country and armed forces with much-needed food rations.

Between 1914 and 1918 the parks were also adopted as training and parade grounds for the new local 'Pals' regiments. Using parks for military training may appear to be a stark contrast to their original recreational function, but there had frequently been a military presence in Liverpool's parks in the form of military bands and regimental parades. In the 1860s, fear of invasion by Napoleon III had caused parks across

Figure 58 *Dating from 1917, this rare photograph depicts crop cultivation in Calderstones Park. [Liverpool Record Office, Liverpool Libraries, Photographs and Small Prints]*

Britain to be used to drill volunteers, and thereafter drilling was perceived as an enjoyable public spectacle. On one occasion, in 1904, visitors to the Children's Festival in Stanley Park were entertained by five different military and police bands in one evening alone. But when war broke out, things became serious. For the recruits involved, the nature of wartime training differed markedly from peacetime parades, but the parks provided suitable terrain for both purposes. The ease with which parks could be adapted for this function meant that the impact upon the landscape was confined to minor and temporary disturbances to the ground. The production of food and the requisitioning of metal railings caused the most visible damage, but many such injuries were repaired or concealed throughout the 1920s.

In contrast to this earlier conflict, the Second World War had a dramatic and long-lasting impact upon the condition and accessibility of Liverpool's urban parks. Over a period of six years, the city's green spaces were completely transformed by a combination of enemy bombing, anti-aircraft defences, decoy fires and trench shelters. Although sport and other recreational uses for parks continued until the official outbreak of war, the parks were seen as an integral part of Liverpool's defences. As soon as war was anticipated, the city prepared for conflict, and by 1938 the Corporation had introduced defensive installations in many of its parks. As the *Liverpolitan* proclaimed proudly in November of that year, 'trenches in parks and other open spaces have already been dug, and are to be extended and equipped as soon as the Government sanctions the work'.[32] Barrage balloons were raised from Sefton Park and, alongside anti-aircraft guns, defended the city from enemy bombers.

Not all wartime uses of open spaces were directly linked to combat and defence. Perhaps the most dramatic transformation of the parks was horticultural, as the city responded to the call to 'Dig for Victory'. In a similar manner to the way in which sites such as Calderstones Park had been cultivated during the previous conflict, large tracts of land were given over to food production. Across the city, parks were ploughed for farming, either as collectively farmed fields or as smaller allotments for the city's residents. At Sefton Park the use of land for agriculture made a huge impact upon the potential for recreation and sport, as entire lawns and sports grounds were cultivated in a patchwork of small vegetable allotments (Fig 59). Nevertheless, sections of the park land were preserved for enjoyment and leisure, providing much-needed opportunities for respite and sociability during an otherwise austere period in the city's history.

Figure 59 *This aerial reconnaissance photograph from 11 June 1941 illustrates the extent of the air defences located in Sefton Park and the large swathe of playing field given over to allotments for food production. [NMR RAF/13H/UK789v72, 11 Jun 1941]*

Figure 60 *The magnificent glasshouse at Wavertree Botanic Garden, erected in the 1870s, was lost to bombing during the Second World War. The original steps and supporting wall can still be seen.*

Temporary civil defences and agricultural strips certainly impacted upon the appearance and use of the city's parks during the war, but enemy bombing caused the most enduring damage to the condition of Liverpool's public parks. In 1940 and 1941, during intensive periods of bombing in Liverpool, park lodges were completely destroyed at Princes and Stanley Parks. Within the parks themselves the fragile hothouses suffered the greatest damage: the glass was blown out of Sefton Park Palm House and the Gladstone Conservatory at Stanley, and the Crystal Palace-inspired hothouse at the Wavertree Botanic Garden on Edge Lane was entirely lost to Luftwaffe bombs (Fig 60). In addition to actual, physical damage, the perceived threat to park features led to the children's dell at Stanley Park being dismantled and stored (never to be reinstated), and the repeated request for metal resulted in the removal of iron fences that had survived similar requests during the First World War. The impact of these precautionary steps and losses to bombing was potentially temporary, but the extent of bomb damage throughout the city meant that during the post-war years parks and open spaces were low priorities for material resources and manpower. With no means of securing parks, a legacy of damaged and unstable structures, and a lack of funds to combat the slow creep of dereliction, Liverpool's parks were left vulnerable to further damage, decay and vandalism (Figs 61 and 62).

Figure 61 (below, left) Fountains are particularly vulnerable to vandalism. This example, in Wavertree Park, has fallen victim to theft, vandalism and decay. [DP031050]

Figure 62 (below, right) The Wavertree Park fountain had three Liver birds supporting the bowl: they were cut off at the foot, depriving the fountain of its local association. [Katy Jones collection]

Figure 63 *The temporary concert stage, Calderstones Park, 1950s. [Liverpool Record Office, Liverpool Libraries, Photographs and Small Prints]*

Although efforts were made to invest in the parks during the late 1940s – including the installation of a giant chess board at Princes Park, a concert stage at Calderstones Park (Fig 63), and a short-lived open-air theatre at Stanley Park – these new attractions could not compensate for the damaged state of many of the original features. Unfortunately for those who had previously enjoyed and utilised them, the parks had entered into a cycle of decline that was to characterise the city's open spaces for the following five decades (Fig 64).

Figure 64 *This stone statue of Souter Johnny in Wavertree Botanic Garden was one of a pair that framed the entrance to the site's enormous glasshouse. Now decapitated, they are a sad testament to the neglect that ensued after 1945. [DP026294]*

Decline and revival

The damage suffered by some of Liverpool's parks during the Second World War was only rectified in a gradual and partial manner. The restoration of the Palm House in Sefton Park was completed in 1953, but in many cases the cast-iron railings which had been removed in 1941 as a contribution to the war effort were never replaced. As a result, both the security and visual cohesiveness of individual parks were compromised. The ravages of Dutch elm disease from the late 1960s onwards wreaked havoc in a number of Liverpool parks, with the loss of over 700 trees in Sefton Park alone; increasing car usage within the parks, particularly in Sefton Park, was seen as destroying the integrity of park landscapes; and Princes Park fell into a very poor condition, with the loss of the Chinese bridge and repeated arson attacks on the ornamental Swiss boathouse. The open-air swimming pool at Stanley Park, which had been built in 1923 by Walter Spencer at a cost of £6,515, was closed in August 1960 and subsequently demolished, although social change may have also reduced the demand for such a facility. The Gladstone Conservatory was stripped of its statuary and tropical vegetation and leased to a private brewery as a pub. Other features suffered from inadequate maintenance or were placed in storage for security reasons and subsequently lost or forgotten, including the statues donated by George Audley for the enjoyment of young children. The boathouse at Sefton Park, although formally listed in April 1975, also became a victim of vandalism and arson and was finally destroyed in March 2002 (Fig 65). In a wider context, the growth in car ownership during the 1970s and 1980s meant that many metropolitan authorities, such as Liverpool, were encouraged to provide greater access to coast and countryside experiences, rather than to maintain public parks, and the increasing emphasis in policy terms on countryside management and the provision of sports centres led to a reduction in core funding for existing parks and open spaces.

From the early 1980s complaints were voiced over the low budget of the Recreation and Open Spaces Department. In 1989 the famous, three-tiered Victorian Palm House in Sefton Park, with its unique set of bronze

Early morning exercise in Sefton Park.
[DP030939]

and marble statues of famous explorers and naturalists (Figs 66 and 67), was declared an unsafe building and closed to the public. Its future was only recently secured by the establishment of the Sefton Park Palm House Trust, by private donations and a successful application to the Heritage Lottery Fund and other agencies for £3 million. The transformation of over 247 acres (100 hectares) of heavily polluted land in the south docks area of Dingle to host the International Garden Festival in 1984, with over 60 individual gardens and a Festival Hall, was undoubtedly a major achievement by the City Council and the Merseyside Development Corporation. However, members of the Militant Tendency were blamed for the failure to capitalise on this opportunity to create a new public park and sports complex as originally envisaged. The Festival was intended to create a unique riverside parkland which would be available for all to share, but the core site has remained derelict for many years. Only recently has preliminary agreement been reached on its partial reinstatement, but the appropriate balance between housing development on the site and open space provision remains contentious.

Liverpool City Council has acknowledged that the overall condition

Figure 65 (far left) *The footings of the boathouse at Sefton Park are the only part of this building to survive. [DP026203]*

Figures 66 and 67 *Around the Sefton Park Palm House stand a series of statues that were cleaned and conserved as part of the recent restoration project. The figures chosen were considered especially appropriate for a site dedicated to horticulture. These include:* (left, top) *Carl von Linné (1707–78), a Swedish botanist, and* (left, bottom) *Christopher Columbus (1451–1506), whose statue celebrates the role of explorers in bringing botanical knowledge and specimens to Britain. [DP030950 and DP026245]*

of the city's parks and open spaces deteriorated in the latter decades of the 20th century, partly because they represented a non-statutory service which often suffered from disproportionate budgetary reductions in comparison with other mainstream service areas. The historic legacy of the public parks movement in Liverpool, as elsewhere in Britain, was further undermined by management reforms in local government, following the Bains Committee Report of 1972, the introduction of compulsory competitive tendering, the sale or demolition of park lodges, and the disbanding of the park police force. The move to compulsory competitive tendering also led to the loss of experienced staff and deskilling, as maintenance regimes concentrated on grass-cutting rather than horticulture. But it is important to remember that the decline of the parks infrastructure in Liverpool, where the appearance of increasing neglect contributed to a reduction in park use and the acceleration of a downward spiral, was very much part of a national trend. To some extent, open space ceased to be a core concern of urban planning, and the absence of any statutory requirement for local authorities to maintain parks and gardens in an adequate fashion accelerated their relative decline at a time of economic stringency and more pressing alternative expenditure priorities. For the United Kingdom, as a whole, the estimated cumulative loss of revenue for funding parks between 1981 and 2001 amounted to £1.3 billion.[33] Indeed, despite increased funding in recent years from both central government and the Heritage Lottery Fund, overall expenditure on parks and open spaces has fallen by 35 per cent since 1991, a trend which reflects neither public preference nor council choice.[34] Liverpool's ability to sustain its historic legacy of parks and open spaces was also severely constrained during the 1970s and 1980s by wider developments, including structural change in the region's economy, high unemployment and political instability. Employment levels in the city plummeted by one-third between 1971 and 1985, while a continued and substantial fall in total population left the city with a civic infrastructure which it could no longer maintain. At a time of significant economic decline and persistent, deeply embedded social problems, it is not surprising that parks and open spaces were not viewed as an important priority on local political agendas.

Although the impact of national trends on the quality of urban green space provision was aggravated in the case of Liverpool by local factors, the profile of parks and open spaces during the period between 1945 and the late 20th century was not entirely negative. Even though Liverpool continued to benefit from its impressive legacy of historic parks and the unique ribbon of open space provision surrounding the city, there was a continuing commitment to create new open space facilities for the general public. In 1950 Otterspool Promenade was opened as one of the few publicly accessible open spaces fronting the Mersey. During the 1960s, the creation of Everton Park was envisaged as an important contribution to urban regeneration in an area of the city known for its poor housing conditions and derelict land (Fig 68). The winning design

Figure 68 *New parks often face similar challenges to their established counterparts. The topography of Everton Park provides visitors with spectacular views across the Mersey, but the steep slope of the site makes accessibility an ongoing issue. [DP026163]*

by Derek Lovejoy and Associates was never implemented and the park was not laid out until the early 1980s, as part of the Militant Tendency's Urban Regeneration Strategy, but it now represents one of the largest expanses of green space within a relatively short distance of the city centre. Despite the failure to develop the International Garden Festival Site as a permanent addition to Liverpool's green space provision, the Festival, held between 2 May and 14 October 1984, attracted over 3.4 million visitors and the range of both national and international gardens was regarded as one of Britain's most important landscape designs of the period.

The acquisition of former estates as new park facilities for the local population, as a result of either purchase or bequest, was essentially a phenomenon of the early 20th century, but Croxteth Country Park, acquired in 1989, undoubtedly represents a significant addition to Liverpool's wealth of parkland. Together, the hall and park, now solely managed by Liverpool's Parks and Environment department, form the city's largest public open space. The hall, dating from the 16th century, is listed grade II★, and the surrounding park of approximately 568 acres (230 hectares) includes extensive lawns, tree and shrub plantations, ornamental woodland, a pheasantry and a brick-walled kitchen garden. Urban regeneration also led to the creation of Netherley Park in 1991–2, while the Fazakerley Ecology Park and the Liverpool Loop Line linear park provide access to different natural environments within the city, in the latter case exploiting the open space potential of a disused railway line to considerable effect in sustaining a more natural, habitat-rich area.

Despite the underlying problems of insufficient funding and restricted maintenance, many of Liverpool's parks have proved to be very robust, and in most cases the original landscape designs have been retained. Moreover, they have continued to fulfil their original function by serving as a focal point for local identity, offering opportunities for relaxation and leisure, and providing sports facilities for a wide range of the local population (Fig 69). In the case of Sefton Park, a number of established sporting clubs have continued to thrive, including the Mersey Bowmen Tennis Club, Sefton Park Bowling Club and Sefton Park Cricket Club, in line with the original by-laws, which only permitted cricket and

Figure 69 *Bowls remain one of the most popular attractions throughout the city, particularly among older residents. The Council maintains a number of greens, including two at Calderstones Park, which are in constant use throughout the summer. [DP026144]*

other 'refined' forms of recreation. In reality, the park has been used extensively, in a more informal fashion, for football, baseball and other sports by both local teenagers and students accommodated in the surrounding halls of residence. In the case of Stanley Park over half of the original site, as designed by Edward Kemp, was originally intended for a variety of sports, but by the 1880s football had become predominant. If the demolition of the open-air swimming pool in 1960 marked the end of one type of activity, the construction of the Vernon Sangster Sports Centre in the 1970s led to the opening of the park's 'least attractive, but most well-used building',[35] and other areas continued to be used for football matches by the local population.

To this extent, parks and open spaces remained an important local resource throughout the second half of the 20th century, irrespective of changing funding regimes and political priorities, although the scale of cumulative under-investment since the immediate post-war period cannot be ignored. Indeed, between 1934 and 2004 the provision of public open space in Liverpool per 1,000 citizens actually rose from 2.47 acres (1 hectare) to 6.67 acres (2.74 hectares): even if due allowance is given for the cumulative reduction in total population, this still represented a real increase in the availability of parks and open spaces (Fig 70).[36]

Figure 70 *Princes Park offers open space, tranquillity and the beauty of nature at all times of the year. [DP030903]*

The revival of Liverpool's parks and open spaces

Until recently, Britain's important heritage of public parks had suffered from obvious neglect. However, in recent years the wider significance of parks and open spaces has again been recognised and an attempt has been made to reverse the pattern of long-term decline, at both a national and local level. The great push for the restoration of public parks came essentially from the grass roots, with the Garden History Society and the Victorian Society playing a critical role. The turning point came with the establishment of a Parliamentary Select Committee, chaired by Andrew Bennett MP, which led to the setting up of a taskforce on town and country parks.[37] Central government has increasingly set the context for formulating overall policy with an agenda influenced by a number of agencies, including English Heritage, the Heritage Lottery Fund and CABE Space, while local authorities have been mandated to develop an appropriate strategy for the restoration, regeneration and maintenance of green space as a key community resource. Research has shown that the British public value parks and open spaces as much as local schools and that good-quality parks are 'essential to the well-being and future' of towns and cities. They represent an important educational resource and can generate considerable social benefits by encouraging a shared sense of civic identity.[38] Access to good-quality, well-maintained public open spaces can contribute to improved physical and mental health, while parks offer significant play and recreation benefits to children and young people. If properly maintained, public parks and open spaces can support urban regeneration, sustain the recovery of local housing markets, and enable communities to achieve biodiversity and urban sustainability within the framework of Agenda 21 and other policy measures designed to tackle the negative effects of climate change.

Many of the arguments for reaffirming the wider significance of urban green space actually reflect 19th-century discourses which underpinned the development of the original public parks movement, but the recent prioritisation of parks was itself a response by central government to the scale of relative decline in the provision and maintenance of open spaces by many local authorities throughout the

United Kingdom. The importance of parks and open spaces for the well-being of local communities has been championed at a national level by a number of agencies, including CABE Space, English Heritage and Green Space, which have helped to establish the extent to which good-quality urban green space can generate economic value in itself, apart from offering significant environmental benefits and providing opportunities for sports and recreational activities which reflect other important policy objectives. Both CABE Space, through its Strategic Enabling Scheme, and English Heritage have played an important role in focusing attention on the need to restore and rejuvenate Liverpool's parks and open spaces. The Liverpool Open Space Study[39] provided a useful, historical assessment of open space provision in the city with a detailed site characterisation of individual parks, squares, cemeteries and allotments, while the report compiled by Alan Barber offered a vision for the future development of parks and open spaces which has had a direct impact on policy formulation.[40]

At the same time, grass-roots support for the regeneration of many of Liverpool's parks has developed considerably with the formation of over 20 Friends groups. The Friends of Newsham Park, for example, has campaigned for the refurbishment of perimeter housing and the partial night-time closure of Gardner's Drive to vehicles, while the Friends of Stanley Park have opposed, without success, the construction of a new football stadium on land which was originally part of the park. Although they are not necessarily representative of all park users and there is considerable variation in terms of the range, size and age composition of their membership, local Friends groups have a very important role to play in safeguarding and developing open space provision, given their commitment to raising the profile of individual parks, to enhancing their use for recreational pleasures, and to facilitating the involvement of the local community in their future management and maintenance.

A number of Friends groups have already achieved a great deal: the Friends of Croxteth Country Park have over 300 members; the Friends of Reynolds Park have obtained funding for a number of community projects, including a Poet Tree Trail; while the enthusiasm and commitment of the Friends of St James' Gardens were critical factors in restoring the cemetery site so that it could be used as a green space for all members of the local community (Fig 71). In conjunction with policy initiatives by central government and the commitment by the City Council to implement a strategy which will support the regeneration of parks and open spaces in line with local needs, the increased involvement of Friends groups and other stakeholders in the management and development of individual parks can only be welcomed.

Current concerns and future opportunities

According to the Public Accounts Committee, in 2006 65 per cent of councils had not completed an audit of green space in line with planning policy guidelines, while over one-third of all local authorities have still to develop a green space strategy which is fully integrated into the planning system in accordance with PPG17, the *Planning for Open Space, Sport and Recreation* guidance.[41] Liverpool has not yet followed the guidelines in full, but the City Council has taken significant steps towards formulating a strategy which contains a vision for 'a network of high quality, accessible parks and green spaces', designed to promote economic regeneration, create a more attractive residential environment, support biodiversity and meet local needs (Fig 72).[42] The underlying objectives were set out in an earlier mission statement, which expressed a clear commitment 'to create a quality diverse network of parks and open spaces'[43] which would help to develop more inclusive communities, safeguard natural and historic resources, promote sustainable development, encourage economic investment, stimulate local interest and provide educational and recreational opportunities.

Such an approach is to be welcomed, particularly in a context where the City Council has been under considerable pressure to accommodate other more powerful interest groups in determining the future use of urban green space. The construction of a new stadium by Liverpool Football Club in the eastern part of Stanley Park has been the subject of intense debate, principally over the loss of public space in what is regarded

Figure 71 *A few years ago, St James' Cemetery was in a run-down condition, but now it is an attractive and valued public open space. This view shows the Oratory beside one of the entrances to the gardens. [DP026267]*

Figure 72 *Small, local parks are often the most popular sites among residents. Greenbank Park has recently been restored and now contains the Marie Curie Children's Garden of Hope (2005) as well as a local graffiti art project. [DP026168]*

as one of England's best Victorian municipal parks. After lengthy deliberation and consultation, Liverpool City Council, supported by English Heritage, permitted the development on the grounds that the benefits of the associated regeneration package – which includes one of the largest park restoration projects in the country, adequate resources for long-term maintenance, and investment in the economy and fabric of the surrounding area – outweighed the loss, serious though that was, to the historic park and to public rights of access (Fig 73). The construction of the Academy of St Francis of Assisi on an underused depot site at the western end of Newsham Park, within the framework of the Government's City Academy Programme, caused considerable concern to many local residents, given the park's status as a conservation area (Fig 74), while

Figure 73 *Liverpool Football Club's new stadium will have a dramatic visual impact on Stanley Park. It is anticipated that public facilities, including a sports centre, will be included in the stadium, seen here in a design drawing.[Reproduced by kind permission of HKS Inc]*

plans to redevelop Alder Hey Children's Hospital, drawn up in association with the Prince's Foundation, if ever implemented, would involve the loss of Springfield Park, one of only a few former country estates in the north of Liverpool which has been preserved as a public park. Although planning permission for the International Garden Festival Site will directly facilitate the reinstatement of sections of the original landscape design, including the Chinese and Japanese gardens, and bring back areas of open space into public use, some members of the local community have actively opposed the over-development of the area for housing and the loss of the woodland embankment on Otterspool Promenade: the proposal has now been referred to the Secretary of State for Communities and Local Government for further consideration. Indeed, according to Councillor Frank Doran, there is considerable concern that future changes in planning arrangements, as envisaged by central government, might 'make it easier for developers to actually build on parks'.[44]

Figure 74 (below) *Building in and around parks remains a contentious issue. The Academy of St Francis of Assisi, recently erected on the edge of Newsham Park, was 'England's number one value added school 2006' but its visual impact upon the park continues to arouse debate among residents. [DP031255]*

However, the parks strategy for Liverpool, formally adopted in 2006, has finally established an appropriate framework for the future development of parks and open spaces. The City Council has now formally placed parks 'at the heart of its regeneration agenda' and it is firmly committed to 'reverse any erosion or deterioration of our park heritage'. Moreover, a series of concrete objectives has been set out which will hopefully protect parks and open spaces from future development threats. Within three years a site management plan will be in place for every 'High Level Park', including all the major city parks on English Heritage's Register of Historic Parks and Gardens and those with Green Flag awards: each of these parks will have its own Friends group. The Green Flag programme provides a national benchmark for measuring the quality of parks and open spaces, and has encouraged the development of partnerships and community links. By 2015 50 per cent of Liverpool's population will live within 500 metres of a Green Flag-rated (or equivalent) park, and there is a clear commitment to apply Green Flag standards to an increasing number of open spaces throughout the city (Fig 75).[45]

The parks strategy is a highly significant document and offers much hope for the future. Its impact will depend, of course, on the future level of local authority funding for the city's parks and steps need to be taken to ensure that resources are not diverted to other purposes. It also expresses aspirations which reflect government and council priorities, but, in the nature of strategic statements, it inevitably leaves open many questions about how policy will be implemented in practice and the future availability of adequate funding for maintenance. How, for example, will young people be helped to acquire a greater awareness of the historic legacy and contemporary importance of parks, and how will the commitment 'to work to improve the maintenance standards on a day to day basis'[46] be managed? A great effort, by the City Council and its partners, will be needed to turn the strategy into reality. Nevertheless, the parks strategy demonstrates a real commitment to urban green space and to the needs of the city's inhabitants that the civic dignitaries of the 19th century would have undoubtedly approved.

In reality, there have been significant improvements in the quality of the city's parks and open spaces in the last few years. The 2005 review of

Figure 75 *Everton Park Nature Garden, opened in 1992, has been awarded Green Flag status.* [Liverpool City Council]

Liverpool's open spaces highlighted a number of cases where maintenance levels were excellent: Calderstones Park was 'immaculately well-maintained', while Allerton Tower and Allerton Golf Course were clearly 'well-maintained'.[47] In 2002, when Liverpool first entered the scheme, it obtained 3 Green Flag awards: by 2007 13 parks and gardens were officially recognised as meeting national benchmark standards, including Croxteth Country Park. The Green Flag scheme has been deliberately used as a 'key driver' in raising the quality of Liverpool's parks, with an increasing number of successful applications representing individual 'building blocks' designed to improve the city's green spaces, and the City Council is recognised as one of the country's leading Green Flag authorities. The first Urban Ranger was appointed in 1984 with a focus on interpretation and education, and there has been a significant increase in the number and range of activities offered by Liverpool's Park Rangers following their introduction in 1993 with the specific objective of promoting the city's parks, open spaces and green environment (Fig 76). All of the city's historic parks have dedicated park keepers. Although there is only an operational base in Calderstones,

Croxteth, Sefton and Stanley Parks, a number of other parks have site-based gardeners within their walled gardens, including Greenbank Park, Reynolds Park and Woolton Wood. It is important to emphasise, however, that the high quality of individual sites such as Reynolds Park has been directly attributed to the hard work of dedicated staff (Figs 77 and 78). Recent improvements in the quality of Liverpool's parks and open spaces have also reflected a more structured and strategic approach to management, the adoption of best practice as defined by national agencies such as CABE Space and Greenspace, and a growing acceptance of the importance of partnerships between the public, private and voluntary sectors in supporting and sustaining their wider community role. To this extent, considerable progress is already being made to restore and regenerate Liverpool's parks and open spaces.

The creation of public parks in 19th-century Liverpool was part of a wider social and political process: they reinforced civic pride, provided a

Figure 76 *Park Rangers lead many educational and recreational activities which bring people into Liverpool's parks: here a special 'pirates' event was held in the Palm House in Sefton Park. [Liverpool City Council]*

Figures 77 and 78 *Gardeners and park maintenance staff are the lifeblood of Liverpool's parks and gardens. However, after decades of underfunding, there is a substantial skills shortage in this sector. Training and retaining staff must be one of the priorities for every parks service. [DP026170 and DP031289]*

range of sporting and recreational facilities for different social groups, and helped to address health and sanitary reform agendas. After almost half a century of relative neglect and decline, Liverpool's parks and green spaces have been recognised again as an essential part of its urban heritage and infrastructure, which provide a sense of place, engender civic pride, promote social interaction, and foster community development. Within this context, the formal commitment by the City Council 'to celebrate the potential and importance' of the city's parks and open spaces and its 'strong commitment' to improve the 'long term wellbeing' of Liverpool's parks represent a further stage in this process.[48]

Learning lessons from the past: parks, open spaces and the public image of Liverpool

The provision of parks and open spaces in Liverpool has evolved through distinct development phases, from the private walks and prospects of the 18th century, to the municipal parks of the Victorian and Edwardian periods, and, more recently, neighbourhood green space and land reclamation sites. As this book has shown throughout this period, public parks have played an integral role in the city's development. Primarily as a result of the wealth created through trade and commerce in the

19th century, Liverpool has an international reputation for its landscape heritage with a large number of parks of historical significance. Sefton Park (grade II★), designed by Edouard André and Lewis Hornblower, was the first public park in Britain to introduce French design principles pioneered in Paris by J C A Alphand, while Croxteth Country Park, Newsham Park, Princes Park, Stanley Park, and Wavertree Park and Botanic Garden are all listed as grade-II sites in English Heritage's Register of Historic Parks and Gardens. Joseph Paxton's design for Princes Park in 1842 was his first independent work for a park and was to be enormously influential in terms of the future development of public park design. Edward Kemp, who had been trained by Paxton and had been responsible for laying out Birkenhead Park (opened in 1847), was commissioned in 1864 to prepare a design for Newsham Park and he also designed Stanley Park, 'arguably the most architecturally significant of the city's great Victorian parks'.[49] Liverpool, therefore, has a unique range of parks of international significance created by some of the most important landscape designers of the 19th century. Moreover, most of these historic parks were designed as part of a ribbon of open space provision created in the late 1860s and early 1870s which has proved to be a unique legacy for later generations.

But individual parks and open spaces are not only important in terms of their historical role in the development of urban landscape design. As in other towns and cities, they represent an invaluable environmental and leisure asset. They provide a distinct sense of place for many local communities; they offer urban children an opportunity to use public space positively with imaginative and challenging play facilities; they enable people of all ages to enjoy an environment which enhances health and welfare; and they encourage a wide range of sporting activities (Figs 79 and 80).[50] But parks and open spaces also have a critical role to play in providing opportunities for exercise, for the implementation of play strategies designed to tackle child obesity, and for tempering climate change. The belated acceptance in recent years that high-quality parks and public spaces help to create economic, environmental and social value simply endorses a point of view which would have been recognised by many 19th-century proponents of the public parks movement.

Figure 79 *New facilities, such as the Linda McCartney Play Area in Calderstones Park (2000), have helped to bring new life and visitors to existing green spaces across Liverpool. Calderstones is 1 of 13 of the city's parks that currently hold much-coveted Green Flag Awards for the quality of the experience offered to visitors. [DP026141]*

But in the absence of any statutory requirement for local authorities to maintain parks and open spaces – in terms of providing the necessary funding for conservation, maintenance and management – the precise mechanism for exploiting their underlying community benefits remains unclear. In this respect, the situation in Liverpool is no different, in principle, to that of other urban authorities. External funding, primarily from the Heritage Lottery Fund, has been obtained for the restoration of historic sites of international importance, such as Sefton Park, but private sector involvement in the regeneration of parks and open spaces, as in the cases of Stanley Park and the International Garden Festival Site, is often more problematic. Other funding models for enhancing the quality of park provision or for repairing and retaining the surviving historic fabric of Liverpool's parks have yet to be explored.[51] Although local authorities have only limited autonomy in raising additional taxes for specific purposes, including the provision of urban green space, the future management of Liverpool's public parks and open spaces will undoubtedly benefit from the developing degree of voluntary and community sector involvement.

Ultimately, greater use and enjoyment of public parks by the local community will contribute to their future success, as they are increasingly recognised and appreciated as a collective asset which reflects the new dynamism of Liverpool itself. The city's current renaissance, therefore, will also depend on a collective commitment to restore, develop and maintain a network of high-quality, accessible parks and green spaces which will both enhance Liverpool's profile as an attractive urban environment and reflect the changing needs of its population. A clear vision for the future of Liverpool's parks and open spaces has now been established in terms of both immediate management needs and long-term objectives. They represent a special resource for local communities and their future maintenance and development need to be viewed as a core public service. An understanding of the historical development of the city's parks and open spaces is important in this context: it will help to raise their profile, reinforce the case for their restoration and enable the city to enjoy again an international reputation for its landscape legacy.

Figure 80 *Angling in Princes Park.* [DP026200]

Notes

1 Moss 1796, 2

2 Stonehouse 1852, 195

3 Moss 1796, 110–11

4 Troughton 1797, 84

5 Anon 1805, 30

6 Garden Committee Minutes, 30 Dec 1857

7 Moss 1796, 22–3

8 Garden Committee Minutes, 24 Apr 1839

9 Cornish 1838, 47

10 Garden Committee Minutes, 8 May 1839

11 Garden Committee Minutes, 9 Mar 1843

12 Anon 1837, 7–8

13 *Liverpool Mercury*, 10 May 1844, 158

14 *The Porcupine*, 29 Jun 1861, 146

15 Trench 1863, 9

16 *The Porcupine*, 29 Jun 1861, 145

17 *The Porcupine*, 29 Jun 1861, 146

18 *The Porcupine*, 21 May 1870, 77

19 Pattern 1902, 104–5

20 *The Porcupine*, 21 May 1870, 76

21 *Illustrated London News*, 28 May 1870, 545

22 *Liberal Review*, 4 Oct 1879, 11

23 Diary of A G Kurtz, 19 Dec 1871. 81 vols, 1841–1890. Liverpool Record Office, Liverpool Libraries, 920 KUR

24 *The Liverpool Citizen*, 11 Jul 1888, 3

25 *Ibid*

26 *The Liverpool Citizen*, 11 Jul 1888, 4

27 O'Mahony 1934, 13

28 Pattern 1902, 94

29 Whittington-Egan 1957, 235

30 O'Mahony 1934, 4

31 *Daily Post and Mercury*, 9 May 1931, 7

32 *Liverpolitan*, Nov 1938, 43

33 Public Parks Assessment 2001

34 Barber 2007, 23

35 Physick 2007, 53

36 Barber 2003, 8

37 House of Commons 1999

38 DTLR 2001; Barber 2003

39 Atkins 2004

40 Barber 2003

41 ODPM 2002 (PPG 17); Audit Office 2006, 65; Harding 2007, 15

42 Liverpool City Council, 2005

43 Barber 2003, 24

44 Liverpool Parks and Open Spaces Project 2006, 14

45 Liverpool City Council, 2006

46 Liverpool City Council, 2006, 50

47 Atkins 2004, 2, 4, 6

48 Liverpool City Council 2006, 7

49 www.liverpool.gov.uk/Leisure_and_culture/Parks_and_recreation

50 CABE Space and CABE Education 2004

51 CABE Space 2006a

References and further reading

Anon 1805 *The Picture of Liverpool: Or, Stranger's Guide.* Liverpool

Anon 1837 *List of the Animals in the Liverpool Zoological Gardens, with notices respecting them.* Liverpool: Ross and Nightingale

Atkins 2004 *Liverpool Open Spaces Study: Historical assessment of open spaces within Liverpool.* Liverpool: Liverpool City Council Report

Barber, A 2003 *Vision for the City of Liverpool's Parks and Open Spaces.* Liverpool: Liverpool City Council Report

Barber, A 2007 'Let's talk money', *Green Places, Journal of the Landscape Design Trust,* **35**, 22–5

CABE Space 2006a *Paying for Parks. Eight models for funding urban green spaces.* London: Commission for Architecture and the Built Environment

CABE Space 2006b *Urban Parks: Do you know what you're getting for your money?* London: Commission for Architecture and the Built Environment

CABE Space and CABE Education 2004 *Involving Young People in the Design and Care of Urban Spaces.* London: Commission for Architecture and the Built Environment

Chadwick, G F 1966 *The Park and the Town: Public landscape in the 19th and 20th centuries.* London: The Architectural Press

Colquhoun, K 2004 *A Thing in Disguise: The visionary life of Joseph Paxton.* London: Harper Perennial

Conway, H 1991 *People's Parks: The design and development of Victorian parks in Britain.* Cambridge: Cambridge University Press

Cornish, S 1838 *Cornish's Stranger's Guide to Liverpool and Manchester … .* London: S Cornish & Co

Department for Transport, Local Government and the Regions 2002 *Green Spaces, Better Places.* Interim report of The Urban Green Spaces Taskforce. London: DTLR

Edmondson, J 2005 *William Roscoe and Liverpool's First Botanical Garden.* Liverpool: National Museums Liverpool

Garden Committee Minutes 1836–58. Liverpool Record Office, 352 MIN/GAR 1/1

George, S 2000 *Liverpool Park Estates: Their legal basis, creation and early management.* Liverpool: Liverpool University Press

Harding, S 2007 'Poor Parks in a rich country', *Green Places, Journal of the Landscape Design Trust,* **33**, 15

Heartwell, H 1842 'Characteristics of Manchester: in a series of letters to the Editor', *North of England Magazine,* Apr 1842

House of Commons 1999 Environment, Transport and Regional Affairs Committee, 20th report. *Town and Country Parks.* London: HMSO

Liverpool City Council 2005 *A Parks Strategy for Liverpool* (draft). Liverpool: www.liverpool.gov.uk

Liverpool City Council 2006 *A Parks Strategy for Liverpool*. Liverpool

Liverpool City Council website www.liverpool.gov.uk/Leisure_and_culture/Parks_and_recreation/Parks_and_gardens

Liverpool Parks and Open Spaces Project 2006 *Interview with Cll. Frank Doran (Lib Dem)*, 15 December 2006 (University of Liverpool, School of History)

Millington, R 1957 *The House in the Park*. Liverpool: Corporation of Liverpool

Moss, W 1796 *The Liverpool Guide; including a sketch of the environs: with a map of the town*. Liverpool

Murden, J 2006 'City of change and challenge: Liverpool since 1945', in J Belchem (ed), *Liverpool 800: Culture, character and history*. Liverpool: Liverpool City Council, 393–485

National Audit Office 2006 Office of the Deputy Prime Minister, *Enhancing Urban Green Spaces*. London: HMSO

Office of the Deputy Prime Minister (ODPM) 2002 *Planning for Open Space, Sport and Recreation* Planning Policy Guidance Note 17 (PPG 17). London: HMSO

O'Mahony, M 1934 *The Parks, Gardens, and Recreation Grounds of the City of Liverpool: Official handbook*. Liverpool: Liverpool City Council

Pattern, L 1902 *A Guide to Liverpool*. Liverpool: Liverpool Libraries and Information Service (2004 reprint)

Physick, R 2007 *Played in Liverpool. Charting the history of a city at play*. Manchester: English Heritage

Public Parks Assessment: A survey of local authority owned parks. Urban Parks Forum, Green Space 2001 Report

SCPW 1833 *Report from the Select Committee on Public Walks*. London: House of Commons

Stonehouse, J 1852 'Dramatic places of amusement in Liverpool a century ago', *Trans Hist Soc Lancashire and Cheshire*, **5**, 192–6

Symes, M 1993 *A Glossary of Garden History*. Princes Risborough: Shire

Trench, W S 1863 *Report of the Health of Liverpool*. Liverpool: Corporation of Liverpool

Troughton, T 1797 *A General and Descriptive History of the Ancient and Present State of the Town of Liverpool*. Liverpool

Twist, C 2000 *A History of the Liverpool Parks*. Southport: Hobby Publications

Whittington-Egan, R 1957 *Liverpool Roundabout*. Liverpool: Philip Son and Nephew

Liverpool titles in the Informed Conservation series

Building a Better Society: Liverpool's historic institutional buildings. Colum Giles, 2008. Product code 51332, ISBN 9781873592908

Built on Commerce: Liverpool's central business district. Joseph Sharples and John Stonard, 2008. Product code 51331, ISBN 9781905624348

Ordinary Landscapes, Special Places: Anfield, Breckfield and the growth of Liverpool's suburbs. Adam Menuge, 2008. Product code 51343, ISBN 9781873592892

Places of Health and Amusement: Liverpool's historic parks and gardens. Katy Layton-Jones and Robert Lee, 2008. Product code 51333, ISBN 9781873592915

Religion and Place: Liverpool's historic places of worship. Sarah Brown and Peter de Figueiredo, 2008. Product code 51334, ISBN 9781873592885

Storehouses of Empire: Liverpool's historic warehouses. Colum Giles and Bob Hawkins, 2004. Product code 50920, ISBN 9781873592809

Other titles in this series

Behind the Veneer: The South Shoreditch furniture trade and its buildings. Joanna Smith and Ray Rogers, 2006. Product code 51204, ISBN 9781873592960

The Birmingham Jewellery Quarter: An introduction and guide. John Cattell and Bob Hawkins, 2000. Product code 50205, ISBN 9781850747772

Bridport and West Bay: The buildings of the flax and hemp industry. Mike Williams, 2006. Product code 51167, ISBN 9781873592861

Built to Last? The buildings of the Northamptonshire boot and shoe industry. Kathryn A Morrison with Ann Bond, 2004. Product code 50921, ISBN 9781873592793

Gateshead: Architecture in a changing English urban landscape. Simon Taylor and David Lovie, 2004. Product code 52000, ISBN 9781873592762

Manchester's Northern Quarter. Simon Taylor and Julian Holder, 2008. Product code 50946, ISBN 9781873592847

Manchester: The warehouse legacy – An introduction and guide. Simon Taylor, Malcolm Cooper and P S Barnwell, 2002. Product code 50668, ISBN 9781873592670

Margate's Seaside Heritage. Nigel Barker, Allan Brodie, Nick Dermott, Lucy Jessop and Gary Winter, 2007. Product code 51335, ISBN 9781905624669

Newcastle's Grainger Town: An urban renaissance. Fiona Cullen and David Lovie, 2003. Product code 50811, ISBN 9781873592779

'One Great Workshop': The buildings of the Sheffield metal trades. Nicola Wray, Bob Hawkins and Colum Giles, 2001. Product code 50214, ISBN 9781873592663

Religion and Place in Leeds. John Minnis and Trevor Mitchell, 2007. Product code 51337, ISBN 9781905624485

Stourport-on-Severn: Pioneer town of the canal age. Colum Giles, Keith Falconer, Barry Jones and Michael Taylor. Product code 51290, ISBN 9781905624362

£7.99 each (plus postage and packing)

To order tel: EH Sales 01761 452966
Email: ehsales@gillards.com
Online bookshop: www.english-heritage.org.uk

Parks and open spaces in central Liverpool, *c*1900

1	St Paul's Churchyard	11 Cathedral Church of St Peter	22 Abercromby Square
2	Pownall Square	12 Clayton Square	23 Site of Myrtle Street Botanic Gardens
3	Our Lady and	13 Site of Ranelagh Gardens	24 Kent Square
	St Nicholas's Churchyard	14 Roscoe Gardens	25 St Michael's Churchyard
4	Exchange Flags	15 Site of St Thomas's Churchyard	26 Great George Square
5	Williamson Square	16 Cleveland Square	27 St James' Mount
6	Queen Square	17 Wolstenholme Square	28 St James' Cemetery
7	St John's Gardens	18 Ladies Walk, Duke Street	29 St Bride's Churchyard
8	St George's Place	19 St Luke's Churchyard	30 Falkner Square
9	St Jude's Churchyard	20 Church of Scotland	
10	Derby Square	21 Mulberry Street Recreation Ground	

Legend:
- Modern landmark
- Garden square, park, open space
- Pre-1906 park, open space
- Place of worship

0   100   500m
0   300   1500ft

[Based on the c1906 Ordnance Survey map]

Parks and open spaces in Liverpool, 2005

KEY

1 Warbreck Moor recreation ground
2 Devonfield Gardens, Orrell Park
3 Rice Lane recreation ground
4 Stanley Hospital Gardens
5 Walton Hall Park
6 Liverpool Loop Line
7 Sparrow Hall recreation ground
8 Canalside Park
9 Kirkdale recreation ground
10 Stanley Park
11 Anfield Crematorium Memorial Garden
12 Anfield Cemetery
13 Walton-Clubmoor recreation ground
14 Circular Road (East and West)
15 Norris Green Park
16 Croxteth Country Park
17 Atlantic Park
18 St Martin's Church Gardens
19 Everton Park
20 St George's Church Gardens
21 Whitley Gardens
22 Grant Gardens
23 Lower Breck Road recreation ground
24 Newsham Park
25 Lister Drive recreation ground
26 Muirhead Avenue Gardens

27 Queen's Drive recreation ground
28 Doric Park
29 Springfield Park
30 Our Lady and St Nicholas's Church Gardens
31 St John's Gardens
32 St Jude's Church Gardens
33 Kensington Gardens
34 Holt recreation ground
35 Allenby Square Gardens
36 Dovecot Park
37 St Michael's Church Gardens
38 Great George Square
39 St Luke's Church Gardens
40 St James' Mount and Cemetery
41 Toxteth Tabernacle Gardens
42 Falkner Square
43 Abercromby Square
44 St Mary's Church Gardens
45 Myrtle Street Botanic Garden
46 Crown Street open space, Edge Hill
47 Wavertree Botanic Garden
48 Wavertree Park
49 Rathbone Road recreation ground
50 St Thomas's Church Gardens
51 Princes Park
52 Toxteth Park Cemetery
53 Wavertree Playground

54 Village Green, Wavertree
55 Northway recreation ground
56 Bowring Park
57 Dingle Park Hill open space
58 Sefton Park
59 Greenbank Park
60 Childwall Woods and Fields Local Nature Reserve
61 Netherley Park
62 Otterspool Park and Promenade
63 Sudley Estate
64 Calderstones Park
65 Black Wood
66 Belle Vale Park
67 Reynolds Park
68 Allerton Golf Course
69 Allerton Tower
70 Clarke Gardens
71 Long Lane, Garston
72 Allerton Cemetery
73 Springwood Crematorium Memorial Garden
74 Camp Hill
75 Woolton Wood
76 Banks Road recreation ground
77 Mill Wood, Speke Local Nature Reserve

Back cover
Alliums in Calderstones Park
[DP026140]